P9-EMG-817

GALATIANS
Letter of Liberation

BIBLE STUDY GUIDE

From the Bible-teaching ministry of

Charles R. Swindoll

INSIGHT FOR LIVING

Chuck graduated in 1963 from Dallas Theological Seminary, where he now serves as the school's fourth president, helping to prepare a new generation of men and women for the ministry. Chuck has served in pastorates in three states: Massachusetts, Texas, and California, including almost twenty-three years at the First Evangelical Free Church in Fullerton, California. His sermon messages have been aired over radio since 1979 as the *Insight for Living* broadcast. A best-selling author, Chuck has written numerous books and booklets on many subjects.

Based on the outlines and transcripts of Chuck's sermons, the study guide text is coauthored by Gary Matlack, a graduate of Texas Tech University and Dallas Theological Seminary. He also wrote the Living Insights sections.

Editor in Chief:
Cynthia Swindoll

Coauthor of Text:
Gary Matlack

Senior Editor and Assistant Writer:
Wendy Peterson

Copy Editors:
Deborah Gibbs
Marco Salazar
Karene Wells

Text Designer:
Gary Lett

Graphic System Administrator:
Bob Haskins

Publishing System Specialist:
Alex Pasieka

Director, Communications Division:
John Norton

Project Coordinator:
Shannon Scharkey

Production Coordinator:
Cheri Liefeld

Printer:
Sinclair Printing Company

Unless otherwise identified, all Scripture references are from the New American Standard Bible, © The Lockman Foundation 1960, 1962, 1963, 1968, 1971, 1972, 1973, 1975, 1977, 1995. Used by permission. Scripture taken from the Holy Bible, New International Version © 1973, 1978, 1984 International Bible Society, used by permission of Zondervan Bible Publishers. Other translation cited are *The New Testament in Modern English* [PHILLIPS], *The King James Version* of the Bible [KJV], *The New King James Version* of the Bible [NKJV], and *The Message: The New Testament in Contemporary English* (Colorado Springs, Colo.: NavPress, 1993).

Guide coauthored by Gary Matlack:
Copyright © 1998 by Charles R. Swindoll, Inc.

Guide coauthored by Bill Watkins:
Copyright © 1987 by Charles R. Swindoll, Inc.

Guide edited and expanded by Ed Neuenschwander with the assistance of Bill Butterworth:
Copyright © 1982 by Charles R. Swindoll, Inc.

Original outlines, charts, and transcripts:
Copyright © 1981 by Charles R. Swindoll, Inc.

An effort has been made to locate sources and obtain permission where necessary for the quotations used in this book. In the event of any unintentional omission, a modification will gladly be incorporated in future printings.

Notice

All rights reserved under international copyright conventions. No part of this book may be reproduced in any form or by any means, electronic or mechanical, including photocopying, recording, or by any information storage and retrieval system, without permission from the publisher. Inquiries should be addressed to Insight for Living, Rights and Permissions, Suite 400, 1065 Pacific Center Drive, Anaheim, California 92806-2126. The Rights and Permissions department can also be reached at (714) 575-5000 or by e-mail at rights@insight.org.

ISBN 1-57972-112-5

COVER DESIGN: Nina Paris

COVER IMAGE: Photographed by Jigsaw 2, used by permission of Picture Perfect, New York, N.Y.

Shackle image photographed by G. Robert Nease.

Printed in the United States of America

CONTENTS

INTRODUCTION

I doubt if there is any greater joy on earth than the joy of being free. And the ecstasy is heightened if a person has once been in bondage, held captive by a power that seems impossible to overcome. Being liberated from such clutches brings pleasure beyond description.

Ask anyone who has been freed from prison. Or someone who was once held restrained behind the iron curtain. Or worse, a victim of demonic oppression who is now free of that awful, frightening influence.

Equally delightful is the experience of being delivered from the paralyzing chains of legalism. There are few more dreadful dungeons! And yet many people today have relinquished their liberty and surrendered to the tyranny of the Law, selling themselves into the very slavery from which Christ came to deliver us. Worse yet, merchants of legalism abound—modern-day Judaizers who prey on unsuspecting Christians.

Paul's letter to the Galatians sets us free. It is a bold statement of liberation, pointing us away from a "gospel" of works and toward the true gospel—the glorious grace Christ provides His own. May our Lord use these truths to free us from human bondage by the liberating power of His Spirit. As Jesus said, "You will know the truth, and the truth will make you free" (John 8:32).

Chuck Swindoll

PUTTING TRUTH
INTO ACTION

K nowledge apart from application falls short of God's desire for
His children. He wants us to apply what we learn so that we
will change and grow. This study guide was prepared with these
goals in mind. As you go through the following pages, we hope your
desire to discover biblical truth will grow as your understanding of
God's Word increases and that you will be encouraged to apply what
you've learned.

To assist you in your study, we've included a section called
Living Insights at the end of each lesson. These exercises will
challenge you to study further and to think of specific ways to put
your discoveries into action.

On occasion a lesson is followed by a Digging Deeper section, which gives you additional information and resources to probe
further into some issues raised in that lesson.

There are many ways to use this guide—in personal devotions,
group studies, discussions with friends and family, and Sunday school
classes. And, of course, it's an ideal study aid when you're listening
to its corresponding *Insight for Living* radio series.

To benefit most from this study guide, we would encourage you
to consider it a spiritual journal. That's why we've included space
in the Living Insights for recording your thoughts and discoveries.
We hope you'll return to those sections often for review and encouragement as you continue to grow in your walk with Christ.

Gary Matlack
Coauthor of Text
Author of Living Insights

ACKNOWLEDGEMENTS

Chuck Swindoll and Insight for Living wish to acknowledge and thank expository teacher and author John R. W. Stott for his work *The Message of Galatians: Only One Way*, published by Inter-Varsity Press.

Chuck relied heavily on this excellent commentary for his series *Galatians: Letter of Liberation*.

GALATIANS
Letter of Liberation

GALATIANS

	Personal Words from Paul	Doctrinal Teaching	Practical Exhortations
	Defense of His Apostleship and Message	**Justification by Faith and Freedom from Legalism**	**Freedom to Love and to Serve**
	Confusion	Works vs. faith	Don't be enslaved.
	Clarification	Legalism vs. justification	Serve through love.
	Correction	Bondage vs. freedom	Walk in the Spirit.
			Bear one another's burdens.
			Let us do good.
	CHAPTERS 1–2	*CHAPTERS 3–4*	*CHAPTERS 5–6*

Occasion	Galatians is an impassioned letter. Paul had heard that the Galatian Christians were falling away from the true gospel of grace and turning to a legalistic approach to salvation. He wished to turn them back to the freedom of salvation by faith alone. In doing so, he argued that not only is the sinner *saved* by grace, but the saved sinner also *lives* by grace. Grace is the only way *to* life and the way *of* life.		
Main Theme	Justification comes by faith in Christ Jesus, not by works of the Law.		
Emphasis	The gospel is authentic (source) 1:11–12	The gospel is superior (defense) 3:24–25	The gospel is liberating (impact) 5:13
Key Verses		2:16; 5:1	

Chapter 1

SET ME FREE!

A Survey of Galatians

Why would a slave, once freed, go back to living in bondage? Why would he willingly place his healed ankles back in the shackles that had scraped them raw? Why would he, having breathed the sweet, pure air of the gospel and felt the warmth of the Son on his soul, return to the dark, dank dungeon of legalism?

That's what the apostle Paul wanted to know about the Galatians. "I am amazed," he said, "that you are so quickly deserting Him who called you by the grace of Christ, for a different gospel" (1:6). This "different" gospel was no gospel at all—but a message of faith *plus* works. It undermined the real gospel, making salvation a partially human accomplishment instead of a miraculous and merciful work of God.

So Paul set out to correct this heresy and encourage the Galatians to hold fast to the message he had preached to them—the Good News of freedom in Christ Jesus.

Before working our way through Paul's liberating letter verse by verse, let's explore its background and get a feel for the book as a whole.

Recipients of the Letter

The name "Galatians" was used to designate two different groups of people. Used in a purely ethnic sense, it applied to a people of Celtic descent (Gauls) who settled in northern Asia Minor (modern-day Turkey). The name was also used, however, in a geopolitical sense for the entire Roman province of Galatia, which included the northern region of Asia Minor but extended southward almost to the Mediterranean Sea.

Scholars have debated for years about whether Paul wrote to the people of the "ethnic north" or those living in the southern region of Roman Galatia. The evidence suggests that Paul wrote to the southern Galatians, since his first missionary journey took him through that region—Pisidian Antioch, Iconium, Lystra, and Derbe (see Acts 13:4–14:28). And Paul consistently referred to the churches he had visited in a geopolitical sense.

So the Galatians were most likely inhabitants of southern Galatia who converted to Christianity during Paul's first missionary journey. Paul probably wrote to them from Antioch after that journey, around A.D. 49, making the book of Galatians Paul's earliest epistle and one of the oldest New Testament books.

The Galatian Situation

Distortion of the gospel. That's what prompted the apostle's letter. Shortly after Paul had planted the churches in Galatia, a group of Jews began to attack his message. These Jews, called Judaizers, had incorporated Christ into their religious system but rejected the idea that He alone saves. As commentator G. Walter Hansen explains, they taught

> that it was necessary to belong to the Jewish people in order to receive the full blessing of God. Therefore they required the marks of identity peculiar to

2

the Jewish people: circumcision, sabbath observance and kosher food (see [Gal.] 2:12–14; 4:10; 5:2–3; 6:12–13). . . .

The message of the rival teachers struck a responsive chord in the Galatian churches. The Galatian converts may have been feeling a loss of social identity, since their new faith in Christ excluded them from both the pagan temples and the Jewish synagogues. So they sought identification with the Jewish people—God's people—by observing the law. . . .

Their focus shifted from union with Christ by faith and dependence on the Spirit to identification with the Jewish nation and observance of the law.[1]

Though written to the Galatians centuries ago, Paul's letter is invaluable to us in confronting distortions of the gospel in our own time.

The Value of Galatians

Galatians brings to the forefront at least three issues that are foundational to our faith.

The Definition and Defense of Justification by Faith

Except for the book of Romans, Paul's letter to the Galatians contains perhaps the clearest and most succinct articulation of the gospel in Scripture. Salvation comes by faith in Christ alone; it is God's gracious gift given to undeserving sinners. This truth is the bedrock of our faith. Our understanding of it can make the difference between a life of spiritual freedom and one of bondage.

The Function of the Mosaic Law

The Law does not save us, because none of us can keep the Law perfectly (although legalists would have us believe we can). Discarding legalism, however, doesn't mean we despise the Law. The Law is good; it has a purpose. God gave us the Law to serve as a "tutor" to show us our sin and drive us to the grace found in Christ Jesus.

1. Reprinted from *Galatians* (IVPNTC) by G. Walter Hansen. © 1994 by G. Walter Hansen. Used by permission from InterVarsity Press, P. O. Box 1400, Downers Grove, Ill. 60515, pp. 15–16.

The Balanced Christian Life: Avoiding Both Legalism and Libertinism

The gospel frees us from trying to work our way to God through rule-keeping. But the gospel also keeps us from drifting into libertinism—taking our freedom in Christ to unhealthy or unloving extremes. As those saved by grace, we are now free to love and obey Christ as well as love and serve one another. We're free—not to do whatever we want, but to do what God wants.

Structure and Style of Galatians

Since Galatians is Paul's response to a specific heresy, the letter is direct, concise, and easy to follow. Sometimes Paul's tone is sharp, sarcastic, even angry. He minces no words in exposing the legalists for who they are.

The first two chapters are *personal;* Paul defends his apostleship and the validity of the gospel he preaches. Chapters 3 and 4 are more *doctrinal,* focusing on the defense of justification by faith and how it liberates from legalism. The last two chapters get more *practical,* as Paul exhorts the Galatians to live out their Christian freedom in a spirit of love and service.

Personal Words from Paul (Chaps. 1–2)

As early as the greeting (1:1), the reader senses that Paul is about to pit the message and authority of God against that of mere humans. The Galatian letter, as we will see, is about choosing between God's effective and exclusive way of salvation and futile, fabricated formulas.

Aghast that the Galatians have abandoned the gospel, Paul calls them spiritual deserters. But he reserves his harshest comments for the Judaizers, calling them "accursed" for preaching a gospel that is no gospel at all.

In order to show that his message is indeed the true gospel, Paul sets out to prove that not only the message but the messenger—Paul himself—was appointed by God. His assignment to preach the Good News came directly from Jesus Himself (v. 12).

Paul's gospel also aligned with the message approved and preached by the other apostles. But even apostles can buckle under peer pressure. Peter, whom Paul confronted publicly, and Barnabas were influenced by the "party of the circumcision" and briefly succumbed to legalism (2:11–14).

But, as Paul clearly teaches, it is faith in Christ, not the keeping of the Law, that makes sinners righteous in God's eyes (vv. 15–21; see also Rom. 3:21–26).

Doctrinal Teaching (Chaps. 3–4)

In this section, having established that his gospel is God's gospel, Paul turns again to the Galatians' defection and draws a sharp distinction between law and grace.

How can those saved by grace, Paul wonders, expect to grow by slipping back into legalism? Having begun by faith, how could the Galatians now depend on their own works? Not even Abraham, father of the Jews, was saved by works. He "believed God, and it was reckoned to him as righteousness" (Gal. 3:6).

The Law, rather than saving us, was given to show us God's standards and our sin (v. 19); it served as a "tutor" to bring us to faith in Christ (v. 24). And it is Christ's grace, not the Law, that made the Galatians—and us—part of the family of faith, where neither race, gender, nor social status provides an advantage. We are all corecipients of the grace of God in Christ Jesus (v. 28).

Understandably, then, Paul was dumbfounded that the Galatians would abandon all this—that they would "turn back again to the weak and worthless elemental things" (4:9). So he pleads with them to "become as I am" (v. 12), that is, free from the Law, and turn back to the message he had preached to them.

Practical Exhortations (Chaps. 5–6)

Having defended both his apostolic authority and the doctrine of justification by faith, Paul next turns his attention to a defense of the life of Christian freedom. This will answer the Judaizers' objections that living by grace promotes lawlessness and loose living.

Having been set free in Christ, the Galatians are to "keep standing firm and . . . not be subject again to a yoke of slavery" (5:1). Because that enslaving teaching—which says that circumcision and other rituals save us—is not of God (v. 8). Like leaven (v. 9), this heresy permeates the church and obscures the doctrine of grace. In some of his strongest language, Paul even wishes the pro-circumcision crowd would fall victim to their own practices and mutilate themselves (v. 12).

No, the Galatians were not set free to fall back under the Law.

5

Neither, however, were they liberated to live licentiously. They were set free to love and serve one another (vv. 13–14) and to display true Christlike character (vv. 22–23). In this way, they would truly fulfill the intent of the Law.

Unlike the false teachers, who want to boast in circumcision instead of the Cross (6:12–13), Paul desires to boast only in the "cross of our Lord Jesus Christ" (v. 14). For it is the Savior who died on that cross—not the practice of circumcision—that creates new life (v. 15).

In closing, Paul leaves the Galatians with what they need most—grace.

> The grace of our Lord Jesus Christ be with your spirit, brethren. Amen. (v. 18)

Christ has set us free. Free from the shackles of legalism. Free to love and live for Him. Free to love and serve others. Are you ready, then, to immerse yourself in the study of this liberating letter? Then let's do it. And let freedom ring!

 Living Insights

Take some time to read through the letter to the Galatians in one sitting. Then reflect on the following questions to help prepare for your study of this rich book.

What passion the apostle Paul has for the purity of the gospel! Why do you think the gospel ranks so high on his list of Christian priorities?

_____

_____

_____

_____

What should we be most concerned about in our churches today? Programs? Numerical growth? Church marketing? Or the clear, consistent teaching of the Scriptures, with the gospel as the foundation and focus?

_____

_____

_____

What do you hope to learn from Galatians about your own walk with God? About what's permissible in the Christian life and what's forbidden? About living free in Christ?

_____

_____

_____

_____

How would you like this study to change you, your church, your family life, your friendships and acquaintances, your overall understanding of Scripture?

_____

_____

_____

_____

Now that you have some goals in mind, turn the page and let's work our way through this letter verse by verse. Oh, and leave the shackles. You won't be needing them where we're going.

Chapter 2

ANOTHER GOSPEL IS
NOT *THE* GOSPEL
Galatians 1:1–10

A mazing grace, how sweet the sound . . . to everyone but legalists, that is.

The message of salvation as a free gift of God apart from human effort isn't exactly music to their ears. It sounds more like fingernails scrapped across a chalkboard or a chorus of alley cats. Legalists cringe at a salvation message that removes human works from the equation.

So legalists have composed their own tune: "Semi-amazing grace *plus* works, how reasonable the sound." What's really amazing about their song is who they get to listen to it. Not just non-Christians, but Christians—people who have already accepted the true gospel. People like you and me.

Faith plus works is a catchy tune. It sounds harmless, even helpful at first. If we listen long enough, we'll find ourselves humming it. Then singing it. Then living it. Then forgetting all about grace.

Both tunes played in the Galatian churches. Paul's message of freedom in Christ came first. But then the Judaizers came along with their blaring concert of self-righteousness, drowning out the sweet sound of the gospel. So Paul wrote to the Galatians to bring back the gospel's liberating melody and expose the legalists' music for what it really was—a slave's dirge.

Let's take a look at the first ten verses of Galatians, where we'll see that the legalists' "gospel" is really no gospel at all.

The Man: Paul's Authority Defended

Paul begins his letter by reminding the Galatians of his authority and who gave it to him.

Paul's Role

"Paul, an apostle" (1:1a). This is more than the author's obligatory identification of himself. From the letter's opening, Paul confirms about himself what his detractors were disputing—that he is as much an apostle as the original twelve.

In their strategy to distort the gospel, the Judaizers first tried to discredit Paul. If they could drive a wedge between him and the other apostles, they presumed, then his gospel would carry no weight with the Galatians.

But Paul was, in truth, an apostle. The Greek word *apostolos* carries with it a distinct authority. It "refers to a person who has a right to speak for God as His representative or delegate."[1] The term, as commentator John R. W. Stott explains,

> was not a general word which could be applied to every Christian like the words "believer," "saint" or "brother." It was a special term reserved for the Twelve and for one or two others whom the risen Christ had personally appointed.[2]

Unlike the false teachers in Galatia, who had appointed themselves to speak for God, Paul was

> not sent from men nor through the agency of man, but through Jesus Christ and God the Father, who raised Him from the dead. (v. 1b)

Paul was commissioned by the Lord Himself. So, right up front, he implies that the Galatians are going to have to choose between two messages: (1) one of human fabrication conjured up by false teachers, or (2) one of divine origin delivered by an apostle.

Paul's Greeting

Paul and "all the brethren" (v. 2a) who are with him, extend their greetings to "the churches of Galatia" (v. 2b):

> Grace to you and peace from God our Father and the Lord Jesus Christ, who gave Himself for our sins so that He might rescue us from this present evil age, according to the will of our God and Father, to whom be the glory forevermore. Amen. (vv. 3–5)

What a greeting! It's the gospel in a nutshell. Salvation comes purely by grace and gives us peace with God. A peace wrought by

1. Donald K. Campbell, "Galatians," in *The Bible Knowledge Commentary*, New Testament edition, ed. John F. Walvoord and Roy B. Zuck (Colorado Springs, Colo.: Chariot Victor Publishing, 1983), p. 589.

2. Reprinted from *The Message of Galatians* (BST) by John R. W. Stott. © 1968 by John R. W. Stott. Used by permission from InterVarsity Press, P. O. Box 1400, Downers Grove, Ill. 60515, p. 13.

Jesus Christ, who died for our sins to take us out of the path of God's judgment and enable us to live for God instead of for "this evil age." All this was according to God's plan, and He gets the glory for it.

How antithetical to the Judaizers' message. People didn't invent salvation, didn't purchase it, and can't take credit for it. Redemption is God's work. To bring human achievement into salvation corrupts the gospel.

The Message: Integrity of the Gospel Affirmed

Abandon a God-centered message of salvation for a human-centered one? Unthinkable! But that's exactly what the Galatians did.

Desertion of the Gospel

> I am amazed that you are so quickly deserting
> Him who called you by the grace of Christ. (v. 6a)

"I am amazed!" "I am astonished!" as the NIV puts it. "I marvel!" says the *New King James*. In our vernacular: "I can't believe it!" or, "You've got to be kidding!" You get the point. The Galatians' desertion of the gospel threw Paul for a loop—not just because they had defected, but because they had done it "so quickly" after their conversion, when he last visited them. That's why, as commentator Donald K. Campbell explains, Paul's opening comments in the Galatian letter are somewhat atypical.

> Conspicuous by its absence is Paul's usual expression of thanksgiving to God for his readers. Instead he vented his astonishment and anger over the Galatians' defection. When compared with the opening of 1 Corinthians this is even more striking, for despite the Corinthians' deep moral defection Paul nonetheless expressed commendation. But here in the face of theological departure he did not express thanks, thus emphasizing the more serious nature of doctrinal apostasy.[3]

How soon we can forget grace. How swiftly, in moments of

3. Campbell, "Galatians," p. 590.

insecurity and doubt, we can go back to believing that our human efforts earn points with God.

Notice, though, that the message isn't the only thing from which the Galatians turned away. They deserted "Him," that is, God. He is the giver, the source, of grace. To abandon the gift of grace, then, is to desert the giver. The Greek word for *desert* suggests a military defection. The Galatians, in other words, had become spiritual turncoats, shifting their allegiance to another message of salvation.

Distortion of the Gospel

Paul exposes this message as

> a different gospel; which is really not another; only there are some who are disturbing you and want to distort the gospel of Christ. (vv. 6b–7)

This other gospel was no gospel at all, Paul says. Commentator Leon Morris explains Paul's use of the Greek here.

> There are two Greek words for "another," and, if they are used strictly, the one in 1:6 means "another of a different kind," and the one here [in v. 7a], "another of the same kind." It may well be that Paul's choice of words reflects a situation in which the apostle was saying that the new position that the Galatians were taking up was the acceptance of something essentially different from the gospel he had preached, while they were saying that there was no essential difference between the faith they were professing and what other Christian teachers proclaimed.[4]

The Galatians, in other words, considered the Judaizers' brand of the gospel a legitimate choice. But it wasn't. It was completely different *(heteros)* from Paul's gospel. As different as night from day, fire from water, a lie from the truth, death from life.

These Judaizers were throwing the Galatians into a state of spiritual turmoil by distorting the gospel (v. 7b). Once you add

4. Leon Morris, *Galatians: Paul's Charter of Christian Freedom* (Downers Grove, Ill.: Inter-Varsity Press, 1996), p. 43.

11

something else to the gospel—be it ceremonial rites, baptism, abstaining from movies, whatever—it stops being the gospel.

Denouncement of False Teachers

So how does Paul respond to these truth-twisting Judaizers? Does he set up a little theological chat with them? Does he dismiss their perversion of the gospel as the innocent errors of inexperience? Does he tell the Galatians to welcome the Judaizers into the fellowship and consider them brothers in Christ who differ on minor points of theology? Hardly.

> But if even we, or an angel from heaven, should preach to you a gospel contrary to what we have preached to you, he is to be accursed! As we have said before, so I say again now, if any man is preaching to you a gospel contrary to what you received, he is to be accursed! (vv. 8–9)

Accursed! *Anathema* in the Greek. Paul is calling down God's eternal judgment on these false teachers. Isn't this a little harsh, though? Was Paul having a temper tantrum and lashing out against the false teachers in a moment of rage? Or was he, perhaps, being a little overpossessive of the Galatians or even jealous of the "competition"?

Some might cite these as reasons, but they're hardly valid. Consider, first of all, that Paul even includes himself in the curse: "But even if we, or an angel from heaven" (v. 8a). This, of course, is a hypothetical condition—apostles and angels do not contort but uphold the gospel. Even so this makes the curse universal, applying to anyone who preaches another gospel. Paul's comments, then, aren't venomous, uncontrolled outbursts directed solely at the Judaizers.

Notice, too, that Paul repeats the curse twice. He is deliberate and controlled in his rebuke. His comments are not the off-the-cuff exaggerations of an emotional preacher.

And when we think for a moment about what false teaching does, we'll recognize the appropriateness of Paul's comments. John Stott reminds us that

> the glory of Christ was at stake. To make men's works necessary to salvation, even as a supplement to the work of Christ, is derogatory to His finished work. It is to imply that Christ's work was in some way

unsatisfactory, and that men need to add to it and improve on it. It is, in effect, to declare the cross redundant: "if justification were through the law, then Christ died to no purpose" (Gal. 2:21).[5]

Besides that, people's souls were at stake. As Stott adds, "to corrupt the gospel was to destroy the way of salvation and so to send to ruin souls who might have been saved by it."[6]

The Motive: Pleasing God and Not Men

Paul goes on,

> For am I now seeking the favor of men, or of God? Or am I striving to please men? If I were still trying to please men, I would not be a bond-servant of Christ. (v. 10)

The Judaizers had apparently accused Paul of currying favor with the Gentiles by teaching freedom from the Law. He was going lightly to get their approval, they said, giving a soft message and holding back harder truths. His condemnation of the false teachers, however, would dispel any doubt about whether Paul minced his words.

> Men-pleasers simply do not hurl anathemas against those who proclaim false gospels. Indeed, if the apostle had wanted to please men, he would have remained a zealous Pharisee and promoter of the Law rather than becoming a servant of Christ. Elsewhere Paul affirmed his purpose to please God, not men (cf. 6:12; 1 Thes. 2:4).[7]

Knowing what God wants. Loving what He loves. Communicating what He wants said. That's how we stand strong for the gospel—not by trying to please people. When our passions align with God's, and when the clear presentation of His grace in Christ drives us, we can champion His truth without fear of intimidation.

Pleasing one God, proclaiming one gospel—that was Paul's passion. May it be ours as well.

5. Stott, *The Message of Galatians*, pp. 25–26.
6. Stott, *The Message of Galatians*, p. 26.
7. Campbell, "Galatians," p. 591.

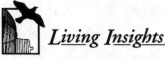

Living Insights

What are you willing to fight for? Your personal safety? The safety of your loved ones? Your country? Democracy? Family values? How about the gospel?

Fighting for the gospel sounds a bit contradictory, doesn't it? After all, the gospel is about peace, not conflict. It provides an escape from divine wrath; it shouldn't stir up wrath. Christians are supposed to be gentle, loving, and agreeable. Right?

Sure, God has called His redeemed to reflect His character, and that includes love, gentleness, kindness, and so on. But it also includes a passion for the gospel's purity. We've already read about Paul's calling down judgment on the Judaizers. But how about our Lord's stinging rebukes of the Pharisees, who obscured grace and tucked it behind a facade of self-righteous rule-keeping?

And how about the Reformation, whose leaders' recovery of the doctrine of justification by faith alone infuriated the leadership of the established church and ignited flames of conflict that burned, often violently, for centuries?

Have you ever heard the advice, "Choose the hills you're willing to die on"? The problem with Christianity in America isn't that we have a shortage of defended hills but that the one hill we should all be willing to die on is conspicuously open to attack—the gospel.

Part of the reason is that grounding believers in the gospel and teaching them the foundational doctrines of grace are no longer the highest priorities in our churches. We have lots of programs, lots of activity, but too few people who can expound and defend the gospel. We need more.

How about you? Take a moment to reflect on your own knowledge of the gospel. If someone asked you, "Hey, just what is the gospel, anyway?" what would you tell them? (See Gal. 1:3; Rom. 3:21–26; 1 Cor. 15:3–4; 2 Cor. 5:21; Titus 3:4–7.)

_____

_____

_____

_____

_____

Would you say that your church leaders are equipping the congregation to recognize false teaching?

_____

_____

_____

_____

If not, what needs to happen for that to take place?

_____

_____

_____

_____

_____

How can you be a part of that change?

_____

_____

_____

_____

_____

Being a Christian doesn't mean we go looking for a fight. But it does mean that when perversions of the gospel seep into our churches, we should be willing not only to teach the truth but also to expose falsehood. Standing up for the gospel invites discussion, even debate at times. And some who despise its message may attack us. But the gospel is a hill worth defending. For it leads all the way to heaven.

Chapter 3

A RADICAL TRANSFORMATION

Galatians 1:11–24

"Heaven's Gate Cult Commits Mass Suicide"
"Federal Agents Slain by Branch Davidians in Waco"

Headlines like these appear much too often these days. They testify to the sad fact that cultic activity is flourishing in the United States, with untold numbers of victims left ravaged in their wake.

In their *Handbook of Today's Religions*, authors Josh McDowell and Don Stewart identify several characteristics common to all cults, one of the most insidious being the "doctrine" of salvation by works. They note:

> One teaching that is totally absent from all the cults is the gospel of the grace of God. No one is taught in the cults that he can be saved from eternal damnation by simply placing his faith in Jesus Christ. It is always belief in Jesus Christ and "do this" or "follow that." All cults attach something to the doctrine of salvation by grace through faith. . . . It is never taught that faith in Christ alone will save anyone.[1]

Herbert W. Armstrong, the founder and leader of the cultic Worldwide Church of God, exemplified this mentality.

> Salvation, then, is a process! But how the God of this world would blind your eyes to that! He tries to deceive you into thinking all there is to it is just "accepting Christ" with "no works"—and presto-chango, you are pronounced "saved." But the Bible reveals that none is yet saved.[2]

1. Josh McDowell and Don Stewart, *Handbook of Today's Religions* (Nashville, Tenn.: Thomas Nelson Publishers, 1983), p. 24.

2. Herbert W. Armstrong, *Why Were You Born?* p. 11, as quoted by McDowell and Stewart in *Handbook of Today's Religions*, p. 24.

16

Many centuries before Herbert Armstrong, Heaven's Gate, and the Branch Davidians, another cult was infecting the church with its version of salvation by works. The Judaizers actively sought to taint the Galatians' minds with the teaching that a person had to become a Jew to be a Christian. Faith in Christ alone was not enough—it had to be accompanied by Jewish ritual and ceremony and adherence to the Law.

To accomplish their goal, the Judaizers attempted to eradicate Paul's gospel by undermining his credibility. They accused him of going too far, saying that his gospel of grace was too easy and enticed people into loose living. Particularly, the Judaizers challenged Paul's apostolic authority, accusing him of preaching a works-free gospel just to win the Galatians' acceptance.

In this chapter, we will see Paul's first steps toward a full-blown refutation of those accusations. He begins by defending his credibility, which upholds the credibility of his message.

Origination of the Message

In Galatians 1:11–12, Paul addresses the Judaizers' first challenge—that his gospel wasn't from God—right from the start.

> For I would have you know, brethren, that the gospel which was preached by me is not according to man. For I neither received it from man, nor was I taught it, but I received it through a revelation of Jesus Christ.

Paul defines the origin of his revelation first negatively, telling his readers where it didn't come from; then positively, telling them where it did come from.

Where the Gospel Did Not Come From

First, Paul stresses that his message was "not according to man," or as the NIV renders it, "not something that man made up" (v. 11). Paul didn't dream up the gospel; it was not his invention. Second, Paul maintains that he did not "receive it from man"—it was not handed down as tradition. And third, he emphasizes that he was not "taught it" (v. 12). He didn't glean it from any human training in the faith, as the rest of us must.

In verse 18, Paul specifically states that he only paused in Jerusalem for fifteen days after a long stay in Arabia. He highlights the

17

brevity of that trip to emphasize that he did not pick up any ideas from the church leaders there. Paul preached his message to people, but it did not have a human origin.

Where the Gospel Did Come From

Then where did Paul get his gospel? He received it "through a revelation of Jesus Christ" (v. 12b). It had been uniquely revealed to him by none other than Jesus Christ Himself. Paul's message, then, was not of mere human origin, but it came directly from God and had all of divine authority behind it.

Today, when people claim to speak for God, we can easily evaluate their message by the standard of the Scriptures. If their teaching is not aligned with God's Word, then we should reject their message and authority.

In Paul's day, however, it wasn't as simple. The Old Testament was the only scriptural authority because the New had not yet been written and compiled. And, though the Old Testament did contain the gospel in veiled form, Paul's opponents didn't recognize it. So he had to prove that this new message of grace was from God. He needed to show that the gospel he preached came from Jesus Christ—untouched by human hands, not manufactured or altered. And he had to demonstrate that he was indeed a God-appointed apostle, authorized to speak for God.

He does just that in the following verses, as he relates the details of God's call on his life.

Transformation of the Man

In this first chapter of Galatians, we see a disturbing picture of a man who killed for his God, a Jew of Jews bent on stamping out what he believed was a blasphemous heresy: Christianity. Then, with arresting speed, Paul's role as the oppressor of the faith was shackled, and he willingly submitted himself as a slave to the gospel of freedom. God's grace turned him around in a radical transformation.

Paul takes us first through the lows, then the highs of his spiritual journey in three phases: before, at, and after his conversion to Christ.

Before Conversion

In verses 13–14, Paul describes his life before he met Christ.

For you have heard of my former manner of life in Judaism, how I used to persecute the church of God beyond measure and tried to destroy it; and I was advancing in Judaism beyond many of my contemporaries among my countrymen, being more extremely zealous for my ancestral traditions.

Paul was a notorious man. He didn't have to explain his past to the Galatians because his former life as a fanatical Pharisee was common knowledge. For the love of Judaism, he viciously tried to wipe Christians out—the King James Version says he "wasted" the church.

In addition to persecuting the "enemy," he was surpassing all his colleagues in "his rigid adherence to the law."[3] He was a religious zealot, steeped in the Torah and in all of the rabbinical traditions that accompanied it. "Thus," commentator Donald K. Campbell observes, "who could accuse Paul of not being acquainted with the teachings of Judaism when he knew them better than the Judaizers?"[4] If anyone knew the value—and limitations—of the Law, it was Paul.

As an aside here, Paul's disposition before his conversion should give us hope for people who appear to be beyond reach. We probably all know someone of whom we can say, "They're too far gone. They'd never be open to the gospel." Yet, in those moments of waning hope, we should remember Paul. Of all people, he appeared to be the least likely candidate for conversion.

And yet, it happened.

At Conversion

Though Paul was running in the wrong direction, God still had a purpose for him; and He stopped Paul cold in his tracks.

But when God, who had set me apart even from my mother's womb and called me through His grace, was pleased to reveal His Son in me so that I might preach Him among the Gentiles. (vv. 15–16a)

3. Taken from *The Expositor's Bible Commentary*, volume 10, edited by Frank E. Gaebelein. Copyright © 1976 by The Zondervan Corporation. Used by permission of Zondervan Publishing House, p. 433.

4. Donald K. Campbell, "Galatians," in *The Bible Knowledge Commentary*, New Testament edition, ed. John F. Walvoord and Roy B. Zuck (Colorado Springs, Colo.: Chariot Victor Publishing, 1983), p. 591.

Did you notice, God set apart Paul, this violent persecutor of the church, to be an apostle—even while he was still in the womb! This is reminiscent of God's call on the prophet Jeremiah's life:

"Before I formed you in the womb I knew you,
And before you were born I consecrated you;
I have appointed you a prophet to the nations."
(Jer. 1:5)

God, in His grace, appointed Paul to preach the gospel in the same way He appointed Jeremiah as a prophet to the nations. The authority of a prophet was something both the Gentiles and the Judaizers could understand. They would recognize that this special calling was initiated by God, not by any human being. So Paul has again affirmed that his calling was divine and that his message had a divine origin.

Next, notice that God was "pleased to reveal His Son in" Paul. In essence, Paul was saying, "God saved me so that His Son might be unveiled in me." God's design for salvation, you see, goes beyond merely saving souls, as miraculous as that is. He created us not only to live with Him in heaven but also to display and glorify Jesus on earth.

For Paul, this call to reveal Christ took him where a devout Jew and Pharisee would never go—to the Gentiles! Only God could have effected a 180-degree turnaround like this.

Because of God's initiative in his life (look at the change of focus from Paul in Galatians 1:13–14 to God in verses 15–16), Paul was finally ready to become a man God could use. So did he go to the other apostles now to learn how to be used of God? No, not even the growth after his conversion could be credited to other people but only to God alone.

After Conversion

Paul next outlines his actions following his conversion. Again, he reiterates that he "did not immediately consult with flesh and blood" (v. 16b). Rather than joining the other apostles in Jerusalem, he instead he stole away to Arabia (v. 17). Mystery envelops Paul's time here. Bishop Lightfoot says, "A veil of thick darkness hangs over St. Paul's visit to Arabia."[5]

---

5. Bishop Joseph Barber Lightfoot, as quoted by John R. W. Stott. Reprinted from *The Message of Galatians* (BST) by John R. W. Stott. © 1968 by John R. W. Stott. Used by permission from InterVarsity Press, P. O. Box 1400, Downers Grove, Ill. 60515, p. 34.

John Stott speculates that

> in this period of withdrawal, as he meditated on the
> Old Testament Scriptures, on the facts of the life
> and death of Jesus that he already knew and on his
> experience of conversion, the gospel of the grace of
> God was revealed to him in its fullness. It has even
> been suggested that those three years in Arabia were
> a deliberate compensation for the three years of in-
> struction which Jesus gave the other apostles, but
> which Paul missed. Now he had Jesus to himself, as
> it were, for three years of solitude in the wilderness.[6]

Eventually, Paul returned to Damascus. In verse 18, we learn
that it was three years after his conversion until he visited Jerusalem,
and this visit lasted only fifteen days. He saw just two of the
apostles—Peter (Cephas) and James, Jesus' brother.

Clearly, Paul's gospel did not come from other people. It came
directly from God. And Paul gives his final proof in verses 20–24:

> (Now in what I am writing to you, I assure you before
> God that I am not lying.) Then I went into the
> regions of Syria and Cilica. I was still unknown by
> sight to the churches of Judea which were in Christ;
> but only, they kept hearing, "He who once perse-
> cuted us is now preaching the faith which he once
> tried to destroy." And they were glorifying God be-
> cause of me.

"Unknown by sight to the churches of Judea"—they only knew
Paul through what they had heard about him. And what had they
heard? That the one who had formerly tried to destroy them had not
only joined them but actively preached the faith! The outcome of
Paul's conversion and ministry was that God was glorified (v. 24)—
the highest affirmation one could ever want.

Stott summarizes the effectiveness of Paul's overall argument:

> The fanaticism of his pre-conversion career, the di-
> vine initiative in his conversion, and his almost total
> isolation from the Jerusalem church leaders afterwards

6. Stott, *The Message of Galatians*, p. 34.

together combined to demonstrate that his message was not from man but from God.[7]

When the Galatians, then, turned away from Paul in favor of the Judaizers, they turned against God Himself.

A Practical Response

Because of everything we've said about the Judaizers, it might be easy for us to look down on them. But just because we're not religious extremists like they were, let's not become too comfortable with ourselves. Evangelicals habitually succumb to a works mentality. Whoa—there's a surprising statement!

We would gasp if anyone told us that we had to ceremonially wash ourselves to be saved, but we sure nurture our own hang-ups. How often do we question the eternal destiny of people who smoke or drink or abuse their bodies? "She's defiling the temple of the Lord!" we say. "How could he possibly be in a right relationship with God." Temple purity. Sounds pretty Judaizing, doesn't it?

So let's really take Paul's message to heart. Let's show confidence in what he preached and proclaim the gospel with all its glorious and grace-filled freedom.

 Living Insights

One lesson we can take from this Galatians 1 passage is that when God transforms a life, there's always a testimony. Though it's the gospel and not our personal story of salvation that brings people into the kingdom, our testimony can provide a conversational framework for delivering the gospel.

Now, for a lot of us, when we hear the word *testimony* we break into a cold sweat. But we really don't need to panic. Giving our testimony is actually quite simple. In fact, the following suggestions can help relieve the pressure.

Things not to do: (1) *Don't preach—just talk.* When you give your testimony, don't make demands or bully the person you're talking to. Let your story speak for itself. (2) *Don't generalize—be specific.* Mention places, events, and people. Share how you felt

---

7. Stott, *The Message of Galatians*, p. 36.

and what you were thinking. Most of all, though, be specific about what it takes to become a Christian; be clear about the gospel. (3) *Don't be vague and mystical—be clear and simple.* Talk straight, and use plain terms. Stay away from Christianese that non-believers wouldn't understand. (4) *Don't defend yourself—just declare your story.* Don't put down someone who argues with you. Just tell your story, and trust in the power of the gospel.

Things to do: (1) *Be brief.* Paul covered fourteen years in thirteen verses. Be specific but also selective; say only what's important. (2) *Be logical.* Follow a logical progression. Tell what happened before, during, and after your conversion. (3) *Be humble.* Glorify God, not yourself. Remember the end result of Paul's testimony? "They were glorifying God because of me" (Gal. 1:24).

Have you ever told your testimony? If so, how long has it been? In light of the preceding clear and simple directions, write out your testimony now. One word of caution before you start: not everyone experiences as drastic a change as Paul. So resist the temptation to create sins or enhance them if you feel your testimony will be boring. The gospel is interesting—and powerful—enough (see Rom. 1:16).

In the space provided, summarize each section of your life. Aim for a testimony that can be given in less than three minutes.

What my life was like before Christ came into it: _____

_____

_____

_____

_____

How I came to know Christ as my Savior: _____

_____

_____

_____

What my life is like now that Christ is in it: _____

_____

_____

_____

_____

Now that you have your testimony together, tell it to someone. You don't have to find a stranger. How about a neighbor or a colleague at work? Write down this person's name, and commit to sharing with him or her within seven days: _____

Remember, you're not giving a presentation; you're sharing your story with someone. It doesn't have to be word-perfect when you give it. Just tell what happened, be clear about the gospel, and let God do the rest.

Chapter 4

A GOSPEL WORTH ACCEPTING AND AFFIRMING

Galatians 2:1–10

If you look at Paul's ministry as a sea voyage, it seems that he rarely sailed along on serene, unruffled waters. More often than not, he coped with waves that would make the sturdiest sailor green with seasickness. What made his voyage so rough? In large part, it came from the constant cannonballing by false teachers, as commentator John Stott explains.

> The bane of Paul's life and ministry was the insidious activity of false teachers. Wherever he went, they dogged his footsteps. No sooner had he planted the gospel in some locality, than false teachers began to trouble the church by perverting it. Further, as we have seen, in order to discredit Paul's message, they also challenged his authority. . . .
>
> One of the ways in which some false teachers of Paul's day tried to undermine his authority was to hint that his gospel was different from Peter's, and indeed from the views of all the other apostles in Jerusalem. . . . They were trying to disrupt the unity of the apostolic circle. They were openly alleging that the apostles contradicted one another. Their game, we might say, was not "robbing Peter to pay Paul," but exalting Peter to spite Paul![1]

Despite the relentless, defaming attacks of his enemies, Paul held his course, steering straight and strong so that nothing would be allowed to capsize the true gospel of God's saving grace.

---

1. Reprinted from *The Message of Galatians* (BST) by John R. W. Stott. © 1968 by John R. W. Stott. Used by permission from InterVarsity Press, P. O. Box 1400, Downers Grove, Ill. 60515, pp. 39–40.

One Gospel

In Galatians 1, we saw Paul proving his apostolic authority through showing the source of his calling: Jesus Christ and God the Father (vv. 1, 11–12). As Eugene Peterson renders it in *The Message*, Paul says, "I'm God-commissioned."[2] Now, in this first section of chapter 2, Paul proves the veracity of the gospel he preaches by showing that he is not only unified with the other apostles but also affirmed by them.

A Revelation and a Journey

Still making it clear that he got his directions from God and not from people, Paul explains why he came to Jerusalem the second time.

> Then after an interval of fourteen years I went up again to Jerusalem with Barnabas, taking Titus along also. It was because of a revelation that I went up. (Gal. 2:1–2a)

Fourteen years after his first visit to Jerusalem, Paul returned to the Holy City and to the foremost leaders of the "mother church."

Scholars debate which visit this was in relation to Luke's record in Acts. The first possibility is the famine visit, where Barnabas and "Saul" were sent by the church in Antioch with a gift for "the relief of the brethren living in Judea" (Acts 11:27–30). The "revelation" Paul speaks of here in Galatians 2:2, then, could refer to the prophecy of Agabus, who foretold the famine (Acts 11:28).

Or this visit could coincide with the Jerusalem Council in Acts 15, where the question of how non-Jews are saved was settled once and for all by the leaders of the church. However, it seems unlikely that Paul would refer to this Council and not use its decrees to refute the charges of his enemies. It also seems improbable that Peter would succumb to Jewish pressure (which Paul confronts him about in our next chapter, on Galatians 2:11–16) after taking such a clear, strong, and settled stand at the Jerusalem Council. In our study, then, we will take the position that this journey of Paul's most likely corresponds to the famine visit in Acts 11.

Paul's companions on that visit were Barnabas, a devout Jewish

---

2. Eugene H. Peterson, *The Message: The New Testament in Contemporary English* (Colorado Springs, Colo.: NavPress, 1993), p. 389.

Christian who was the first to accept Paul after his conversion as well as his first partner in ministry (see Acts 9:26–27; 11:22–30; chaps. 13–14), and Titus, an uncircumcised Gentile convert to Christianity. Titus was sort of a test case—would the other apostles agree with Paul that salvation comes through faith in Christ alone, apart from circumcision, or would they agree with his Judaizing opponents?

With this issue burning in his mind, Paul

> submitted to them the gospel which I preach among the Gentiles, but I did so in private to those who were of reputation, for fear that I might be running, or had run, in vain. (Gal. 2:2b)

For fear that he had run in vain? Was Paul really afraid that he had taught the wrong gospel all these years after all? Not likely—not after having called the preachers of the "different gospel" accursed! Eugene Peterson clarifies Paul's meaning for us as he paraphrases the apostle's words:

> At that time I placed before them exactly what I was preaching to the non-Jews. I did this in private with the leaders, those held in esteem by the church, so that our concern would not become a controversial public issue, marred by ethnic tensions, exposing my years of work to denigration and endangering my present ministry.[3]

In essence, Paul "feared that his past and present ministry might be hindered or rendered of no effect by the Judaizers"[4] if the church leaders did not stand for the gospel of grace that he, like they, had received from Jesus Christ.

How did "those who were of reputation" respond?

> But not even Titus, who was with me, though he was a Greek, was compelled to be circumcised. (v. 3)

Hallelujah! The true gospel was affirmed.

---

3. Peterson, *The Message*, p. 390.

4. Donald K. Campbell, "Galatians," in *The Bible Knowledge Commentary*, New Testament edition, ed. John F. Walvoord and Roy B. Zuck (Colorado Springs, Colo.: Chariot Victor Publishing, 1983), p. 593.

Standing Firm against the Enemy

What exactly was at stake? And what was at the root of the problem? Paul explains in the bluntest of terms.

It was because of the false brethren secretly brought in, who had sneaked in to spy out our liberty which we have in Christ Jesus, in order to bring us into bondage. (v. 4)

Look at his word choices: "false brethren," "secretly," "sneaked," "spy," "bondage." These words, as commentator James Montgomery Boice notes, are a "military metaphor, used to indicate the subversive and militant nature of the evil that Paul was fighting."[5] Paul was in the midst of a deadly battle that held an eternal outcome. Spies who were pretending to be Christians had infiltrated the church, intent on destroying the freedom Christ had purchased for His people. They wanted to chain the Christians as slaves to a futile system of self-righteousness.

For this reason, Paul

did not yield in subjection to them for even an hour, so that the truth of the gospel would remain with you. (v. 5)

The true gospel, which he had received from Jesus Christ Himself, was all that mattered to Paul. He would endure any hardship, face any persecution, and go up against any person—exalted or humble—who would dare to obscure the grace of God with the pride of human works.

Different Yet Equal Ministries

Paul now shifts his attention to his allies and their status. In verse 2, he called them "those who were of reputation"; in verse 6, he calls them "those who were of high reputation"; and in verse 9 he identifies them as James, Peter, and John, "who were reputed to be pillars."

Why does he focus on who they were "reputed" to be? Is this a subtle put-down of these men? Not likely, because that would be

5. Taken from *The Expositor's Bible Commentary*, volume 10, edited by Frank E. Gaebelein. Copyright © 1976 by The Zondervan Corporation. Used by permission of Zondervan Publishing House, p. 440.

divisive. It seems more probable that the Judaizers had exalted these three as "real apostles," in contrast to what they thought of Paul. These three had known Christ in the flesh; Paul had not. They were true apostles; Paul, to them, was self-appointed. They ministered primarily to Jews; Paul brought the "unclean" into the church and let them stay "unclean." The leaders would surely get rid of Paul, the Judaizers must have thought. But what a surprise they got when these leaders not only accepted Titus as he was in Christ but also affirmed Paul's distinctive ministry!

> But from those who were of high reputation (what they were makes no difference to me; God shows no partiality)—well, those who were of reputation contributed nothing to me. (v. 6)

Rather than being intimidated by high reputations, Paul looked at the situation from God's perspective and kept focused on what was important: the truth of the gospel. He knew his message had come from God, and the leaders saw it as well. So they didn't change a thing.

"On the contrary," Paul continues,

> seeing that I had been entrusted with the gospel to the uncircumcised, just as Peter had been to the circumcised (for He who effectually worked for Peter in his apostleship to the circumcised effectually worked for me also to the Gentiles), and recognizing the grace that had been given to me, James and Cephas and John, who were reputed to be pillars, gave to me and Barnabas the right hand of fellowship, so that we might go to the Gentiles and they to the circumcised. (vv. 7–9)

To his enemies' consternation, Paul was accepted as an equal by the other apostles—Peter in particular. Not only that, but these "pillars" recognized that one God was directing their different ministries, one grace was empowering their different missions, and one gospel was the driving force in everything they did.

As a result, they gave Paul and Barnabas the "right hand of fellowship," which was a "sign of agreement and trust and an indication to all present that they endorsed the division of labor."[6] They

6. Campbell, "Galatians," p. 594.

29

were partners, united in vision and mission, unified in the message of salvation.

The Gospel Lived Out

Once Paul, Barnabas, James, Peter, and John had all agreed on what the true gospel was, they wanted to make sure that it didn't become just a static definition. The gospel is dynamic, a vibrant part of our actions and relationships. God's love changes us so that we love and care for the needs of others, which is why Paul records,

> They only asked us to remember the poor—the very thing I also was eager to do. (v. 10)

Commentator Donald Campbell sees an added benefit in this counsel:

> Such offerings would alleviate human suffering, but they would also demonstrate genuine concern on the part of Gentile Christians for Jewish Christians. This in turn would help promote unity and love among believers and help prevent the kinds of misunderstandings which were undermining the Galatian churches.[7]

A worthy goal indeed.

Concluding Thoughts

Isn't it amazing how a debate that took place nearly two thousand years ago is still relevant today? James Montgomery Boice crystallizes the transcendent significance of Paul's stand for the gospel.

> It is to Paul's steadfastness in conflict that Christians owe, humanly speaking, the continuation of the full gospel of grace in subsequent church history. The issue is important today because many would claim that doctrine is not of great importance, that compromise should always be sought, and that the value of human works alongside the reality of grace should be recognized.[8]

7. Campbell, "Galatians," p. 594.
8. *The Expositor's Bible Commentary*, vol. 10, p. 438.

"We did not give in to them for a moment," Paul wrote, "so that the truth of the gospel might remain with you" (v. 5 NIV). What is this gospel? That God's acceptance of us depends solely on His grace—the grace of His Son's substitutionary payment of our sins on the cross that we accept by faith. Plus . . . nothing. It is His gift, His provision, His grace.

That's a gospel worth accepting. That's a gospel worth affirming.

 Living Insights

The gospel, as Paul concluded in Galatians 2:10, is not a tidy summary statement that is meant to stay in our heads. It is meant to be lived relationally. We are to care for those in need. We are to set each other free in Christ rather than cage one another in with our own rules and regulations. We are to affirm the validity of a fellow Christian's mission—even when it is different from our own. And we are to accept one another as God has accepted us.

That last one can get a little sticky, can't it? Downright convicting. It's hard to accept people who lead very different lives from ours. We can feel threatened, that somehow they are doing something we ought to be doing, like moving to the mission field. Or we can feel that they are wrong. Period. Weird. Period. Crazy. Period. Our periods stop our minds and our hearts, bringing our spirits to a screeching halt.

How can we learn to be more accepting? Perhaps a good place to start is considering those people who have accepted us. Those who have affirmed us and given us the right hand of fellowship. Who would that be in your life?

_____

Have you ever told that person (or people) what his or her acceptance has meant to you? If you can contact them, why not write them a letter to thank them for accepting you? And don't forget to thank God for bringing this person into your life.

As you mull over what it means to be an accepting person, like the person who accepted you, consider these illuminating words from Gladys M. Hunt.

> *Acceptance*. It means you are valuable just as you are. It allows you to be the *real* you. You aren't forced

into someone else's idea of who you really are. It means your ideas are taken seriously since they reflect you. You can talk about how you feel inside and why you feel that way—and someone really cares.

Acceptance means you can try out your ideas without being shot down. You can even express heretical thoughts and discuss them with intelligent questioning. You feel safe. No one will pronounce judgment on you, even though they don't agree with you. It doesn't mean you will never be corrected or shown to be wrong; it simply means it is safe to be *you* and no one will destroy *you* out of prejudice.[9]

9. Gladys M. Hunt, "That's No Generation Gap," in *Eternity*, October 1969, p. 15.

Chapter 5
CONFRONTING HYPOCRISY
Galatians 2:11–16

No one is immune to the allure of legalism, with its glittering promise of membership in the holier-than-thou club. Not me. Not you. Not even someone you'd think would surely know better—like the apostle Peter.

Devoted as he was to the Lord, as stalwart a champion as he was for the gospel, Peter, the Rock, briefly succumbed to legalism during his ministry. His actions betrayed his words, contradicting the gospel he so vigorously preached. And by his example, he unwittingly led others away from the freedom of grace and into the bondage of works.

If we're to loosen legalism's grip on the church, we must hold on tight to the true gospel. We must know it. Believe it. Teach it. And, as Paul demonstrates in our Galatians passage, we must be willing to confront those who obscure or contradict it—even if they happen to be prominent Christian leaders.

Why Are These Verses in Galatians?

What does Galatians 2:11–16 have to do with Paul's defense of the gospel and his authority to preach it? Is he diverting from his main topic just to vent some of his frustrations with Peter? Not at all. In fact, Paul's encounter with Peter actually bolsters his argument.

Paul, remember, has been defending his apostleship to the Galatians, emphasizing that his gospel came directly from Jesus, not from human teachers. Even so, Paul's gospel was the same message approved and proclaimed by the other apostles.

Still, the Galatians or Paul's opponents might not have accepted his apostleship or the validity of his message at this point in the letter. So Paul recounts his experience with Peter in Antioch to show how he used his God-given authority to confront another great Christian leader.

When Peter's actions in Antioch contradicted the gospel, Paul confronted him as an equal about his hypocrisy. What a sobering task! But a necessary one, for the preservation of the gospel was at stake. Paul's inclusion of this event in the letter was intended to leave no doubt that he preached the true gospel and possessed the authority to uphold it.

What Occurred . . . and When?

What specifically did Peter do to invoke a rebuke from Paul? First, to understand the magnitude of Peter's lapse, we must go back to Acts 10, where the one-time fisherman had to face the fact that his Jewish, Law-drenched tradition was keeping him from being the "fisher of men" God had intended.

An Encounter with Cornelius

While staying with Simon the tanner[1] in Joppa, Peter

> fell into a trance; and he saw the sky opened up, and an object like a great sheet coming down, low-ered by four corners to the ground, and there were in it all kinds of four-footed animals and crawling creatures of the earth and birds of the air. A voice came to him, "Get up, Peter, kill and eat!" But Peter said, "By no means, Lord, for I have never eaten anything unholy and unclean." Again a voice came to him a second time, "What God has cleansed, no longer consider unholy." This happened three times, and immediately the object was taken up into the sky. (Acts 10:10b–16)

Peter was perplexed, but the mystery was about to unravel. While he was reflecting on the vision, three men sent by God showed up at Simon's place. Greeting Peter, they said,

> "Cornelius, a centurion, a righteous and God-fearing man well spoken of by the entire nation of the Jews,

---

1. "Occupations were frequently used with personal names to identify individuals further (see 16:14; 18:3; 19:24; 2 Ti 4:14), but in this case it is especially significant. A tanner was involved in treating the skins of dead animals, thus contacting the unclean according to Jewish law; so he was despised by many. Peter's decision to stay with him shows already a will-ingness to reject Jewish prejudice and prepares the way for his coming vision and the mission to the Gentiles." Lewis Foster, note on Acts 9:43, in *The NIV Study Bible*, ed. Kenneth L. Barker and others (Grand Rapids, Mich.: Zondervan Bible Publishers, 1985), p. 1662.

was divinely directed by a holy angel to send for you to come to his house and hear a message from you." (v. 22)

Cornelius was a Gentile, considered "unclean" by the Jews. No good Jew would defile himself by going to the house of a Gentile. And Cornelius was a *Roman* Gentile—a centurion, part of the oppressive military establishment that had its black boot on the neck of the Jews.

But, as God had told Peter in his rooftop vision, he was to consider nothing unclean that God had declared clean. God wanted Peter to take the gospel to the home of Cornelius and to the Gentiles.

When Peter preached Christ to all the people assembled in the centurion's house, the Spirit came upon the listeners, and they spoke in tongues—just as the Jews had done at Pentecost. These new Gentile believers were baptized, and Peter stayed with them for a few days (vv. 44–48).

When some of the Jews heard the news, they "took issue" with Peter when he came to Jerusalem (11:2). So he explained his vision and visit to Cornelius' house, concluding,

> "Therefore if God gave to them the same gift as He gave to us also after believing in the Lord Jesus Christ, who was I that I could stand in God's way?" (v. 17)

Who, indeed, can argue with the mighty work of God?

> When they heard this, they quieted down and glorified God, saying, "Well then, God has granted to the Gentiles also the repentance that leads to life." (v. 18)

God's message was clear: Salvation in Jesus Christ was as much for the Gentiles as it was for the Jews. These new believers were no longer "unclean" but corecipients of the grace of God. As new creations in Christ, Jew and Gentile were now part of the same family (see Gal. 3:28).

What a major turning point in the life of the church! Today we would say Peter and the other Jewish Christians experienced a "paradigm shift," a totally new perspective on the Christian life. Jews who would not eat with Gentiles or even enter their homes could now embrace them as brothers and sisters in Christ.

Peter's Lapse at Antioch

This open-armed stance toward Gentiles, however, wasn't accepted right away by all the Jews. The leaders of the church in Jerusalem continued to deal with the issue as problems arose. Then, in a meeting of James, Peter, John, and Paul, Peter openly affirmed the gospel Paul was preaching to the Gentiles (see Gal. 2:1–10).

Peter seemed to have embraced wholeheartedly this new freedom and fellowship with the Gentiles. Dispensing with Jewish dietary laws, he "used to eat with the Gentiles" at Antioch, Paul's home church (Gal. 2:12). Commentator John R. W. Stott explains that Peter's

> old Jewish scruples had been overcome. He did not consider himself in any way defiled or contaminated by contact with uncircumcised Gentile Christians, as once he would have done. Instead, he welcomed them to eat with him, and he ate with them. Peter, who was a Jewish Christian, enjoyed table-fellowship with the Antiochene believers, who were Gentile Christians. This probably means that they had ordinary meals together, although doubtless they partook together of the Lord's Supper as well.[2]

Sometimes, though, circumstances try to convince us that the old way is the best way. And even apostles can give in to the pressure.

Representatives of the Jerusalem church also came to Antioch,[3] but rather than celebrating Christ's grace, they held that the Gentiles must be circumcised to be saved and that they were still unclean and could not eat with Jews (v. 12). Intimidated by their forcefulness, Peter gradually withdrew from the Gentiles, and even Barnabas was "carried away by their hypocrisy" (v. 13).

What are we to make of this? Are we to believe that Peter, after receiving a direct revelation from the Lord and after seeing God's confirming miracle at the house of Cornelius, was now rejecting

---

2. Reprinted from *The Message of Galatians* (BST) by John R. W. Stott. © 1968 by John R. W. Stott. Used by permission from InterVarsity Press, P. O. Box 1400, Downers Grove, Ill. 60515, p. 50.

3. Stott sees these representatives from Jerusalem as self-appointed delegates who came to Antioch—without the authority of James, the leader of the Jerusalem church (see Acts 15:24).

the gospel? Was Peter now a full-fledged legalist who believed that works must accompany faith to secure salvation?

Of course not. Peter's writings confirm that he held fast to the gospel, and history tells us he was martyred for his faith. Yet this once he did succumb to pressure. Out of fear of reproof from influential Jews, he acted contrary to his beliefs.

Though he didn't abandon the faith, Peter's actions were still serious. He was sending mixed signals to the Gentile believers. He was blurring the message of the gospel and obscuring the freedom it provides. Paul recognized that the gospel and the future of the church were at stake.

Paul's Rebuke of Peter

Paul "opposed [Peter] to his face, because he stood condemned" (v. 11). Since Peter's infraction was public, Paul confronted him publicly—"in the presence of all" (v. 14a). He said to Peter,

> "If you, being a Jew, live like the Gentiles and not
> like the Jews, how is it that you compel the Gentiles
> to live like Jews?" (v. 14b)

In other words, "Peter, you certainly haven't been acting like a Jew. You've been eating ham sandwiches with the Gentiles. And now, suddenly, you expect the Gentiles to behave like Jews?"

Commentators vary on whether Paul's rebuke ends at verse 14 or continues to the end of the chapter. No one knows for sure. Whatever the case, we can be certain that the subsequent verses provide the theological reason behind Paul's rebuke: Sinners are declared righteous (justified) by God through faith in Christ, not by keeping the Law (vv. 15–16).

The Outcome

How did Peter respond to Paul's rebuke? The passage doesn't say, and the event is described nowhere else in Scripture. Perhaps the absence of Peter's words in this passage indicates that he listened to Paul, that he knew Paul was right, and that he responded with maturity to the rebuke of his colaborer in the gospel.

We do know that, at the Jerusalem Council, which convened to discuss the issue of whether Gentiles had to be circumcised to be saved, Peter spoke out in favor of releasing the Gentiles from the yoke of the Law and recognizing them as corecipients of God's grace (see Acts 15:6–11). He and Paul were unified on this, as was the entire council, which issued an official statement mandating that the Law not be imposed upon the Gentiles (vv. 19–29).

Peter didn't waffle at the Jerusalem Council. Rather, he publicly opposed those believers who were formerly Pharisees and their demand for circumcision for salvation (v. 5). Since most commentators agree that the council meeting in Acts 15 convened after Paul confronted Peter at Antioch, it appears that Peter did indeed leave his hypocrisy behind.

That should be a great encouragement to us. We're all tempted to succumb to peer pressure and lapse into behavior that contradicts our beliefs. But that doesn't have to take us out of ministry. We can come around. God can still use us. But sometimes it takes a Paul—someone passionate enough about God's grace to confront when it's distorted—to get us back on track.

Some Concluding Applications

What else can we take to heart and put to work from this incident? At least four truths stand out.

First, *we're accountable to other Christians for what we say and do.* The gospel makes us free, but that doesn't mean we're free to live irresponsibly or distort the gospel message. And, though Christians aren't meant to serve as a secret squad of "lifestyle police," we need to keep our eyes and ears open and be willing to speak the truth in love to those who misrepresent the gospel.

Second, *our words and actions have consequences beyond ourselves.* We're all part of God's family. We are "members one of another" (Rom. 12:5). Whether we realize it or not, how we live affects others in the family. This is especially important for you who are influential Christian leaders to remember. People hang on your words and look to you for encouragement and direction. Above all, your life and message should be Christ-centered.

Third, *the gospel must be not only taught but applied.* A person who talks about grace but lives either legalistically or licentiously is a hindrance to the gospel. Have you ever heard the axiom, "What you do speaks so loudly, I cannot hear what you say"? That's especially true in the Christian life.

Fourth, *holiness is our standard.* Since we belong to God, He has called us to live as though we belong to Him. And that's not a message of legalism; it's one of grace. None of us measures up to

God's perfect standards. None of us is capable of loving Him and each other as we should. That is why we need Jesus Christ. Made right with God by Christ's blood, we can walk with God, grow in grace, and display our dependence on Him—whether teaching, preaching, confronting . . . or failing.

It is the gospel, the message of the finished work of Christ, that advances us toward holiness and rescues us from hypocrisy. Just ask Peter. His two biggest blunders—denying Christ and distorting the gospel—are recorded for all to see. But so are all the times he stood strong for his Lord, suffered for Him, and preached His gospel in the power of the Holy Spirit.

 Living Insights

It's not always easy to stand up for what we believe. Fear of rejection by friends or intimidation by people in authority can make us do strange things. We've probably all walked away from an "on the spot" situation and said, "I can't believe I did that" or, "If I had only said . . ." Part of growing in Christ, however, is learning from our mistakes.

Can you think of a time when you succumbed to pressure and acted contrary to your beliefs? When was it?

_____

_____

_____

Did anyone bring your actions to your attention at the time, or did you realize what you had done on your own?

_____

What did you learn from your experience? If the same situation came up today, what would you do differently? How can you prepare for the next time?

_____

_____

_____

Since then, how has God demonstrated His forgiveness and His willingness to continue to use you in His work?

_____

_____

_____

Why not take a moment to thank Him in prayer for His goodness and faithfulness—even when we fail Him.

Chapter 6

THE EXCHANGED LIFE

Galatians 2:17–21

By exposing Peter's hypocrisy, Paul confirmed the truth of the gospel and affirmed his apostolic authority. That should have convinced the Galatians that grace, not the Law, is the way of righteousness and the path to God. Right?

Apparently not. As we pick up in verse 17 and read to the end of chapter 2, it's obvious that Paul anticipates further objections from his readers. So he answers these potential objections and shows once again that the gospel is superior to the Law—not only for entering the Christian life but for living it.

Does Grace Make Christ a Minister of Sin?

Paul knew all too well the objections bouncing around in the brains of his readers. It could be that he voiced the same ones as a staunch Pharisee observing this "lawless" movement called Christianity. Now, though, he asks the question as one saved by grace and placed in union with Jesus Christ—and he provides an inspired answer.

> "But if, while seeking to be justified in Christ, we ourselves have also been found sinners, is Christ then a minister of sin? (2:17a)

John R. W. Stott provides some insight into the assumptions of those who would ask this question.

> Paul's critics argued like this: "Your doctrine of justification through faith in Christ only, apart from the works of the law, is a highly dangerous doctrine. It fatally weakens a man's sense of moral responsibility. If he can be accepted through trusting in Christ, without any necessity to do good works, you are actually encouraging him to break the law, which is the vile heresy of 'antinomianism.'" People still argue like this today: "If God justifies bad people,

what is the point of being good? Can't we do as we like and live as we please?"[1]

Paul's opponents thought that people who disregarded the Law and its righteous works would be "found sinners." And since Christ is the One who supplies this grace that leads to lawlessness, He is actually enabling a sinful lifestyle—He is a "minister of sin."

Is this a valid conclusion to draw from the gospel's message of freedom? "May it never be!" exclaims Paul (v. 17b). *"Mē genoito!"* in the Greek. Paul uses this emphatic statement fourteen times in the New Testament, usually to express his "abhorrence of an inference which he fears may be (falsely) drawn from his argument."[2] Paul is saying, in essence, "If a person is saved by faith alone, apart from works of the Law, does it follow that a sinful lifestyle will result, thus reflecting negatively on Christ? Absolutely not!"

Why is that a false premise? Why doesn't justification by faith alone lead to a sinful life? Paul continues,

"For if I rebuild what I have once destroyed, I prove myself to be a transgressor." (v. 18)

This is a complex verse. Commentator F. F. Bruce sees Paul's phrase "If I rebuild what I have once destroyed" as referring to anyone who, after embracing the gospel, returns to the Law to gain God's favor.

If the law was still in force, as the Galatians were being urged to believe, then those who sought salvation elsewhere were transgressors by its standard; if it was no longer in force—if Christ occupied the place which was now rightly his in salvation history—then those who sought their justification before God anywhere but in Christ remained unjustified, that is to say, they were still in their sins. It is the latter contingency that Paul has in mind as he writes to the Galatians.[3]

1. Reprinted from *The Message of Galatians* (BST) by John R. W. Stott. © 1968 by John R. W. Stott. Used by permission from InterVarsity Press, P. O. Box 1400, Downers Grove, Ill. 60515, p. 64.

2. E. de W. Burton, *Syntax of the Moods and Tenses in New Testament Greek* (Edinburgh, 1955), p. 177; as quoted by Leon Morris in *Galatians: Paul's Charter of Christian Freedom* (Downers Grove, Ill.: InterVarsity Press, 1996), p. 88.

3. F. F. Bruce, *The Epistle to the Galatians: A Commentary on the Greek Text*, The New International Greek Testament Commentary Series (1982; reprint, Exeter, England: Paternoster Press; Grand Rapids, Mich.: William B. Eerdmans Publishing Co., 1990), p. 142.

Amazing, isn't it—the futility of self-righteousness? To us, our best efforts may seem like a sturdy enough staircase to ascend to God. But, like rotten wood, they can't hold us. We can't even take the first step toward heaven without its snapping into splinters beneath us.

Jesus Christ is our only secure staircase. He alone has fulfilled the obligations of the Law on our behalf and made us right with God. Without Him, we are doomed to stumble and tumble in our sin and eventually fall over the railing into the abyss of God's judgment.

Dead to the Law, Alive to God

The Law, however, no longer condemns to death those who are in Christ (see Rom. 8:1). We are, instead, alive to God in Christ. As Paul says,

> "For through the Law I died to the Law, so that I might live to God." (Gal. 2:19)

What a statement for Paul, a one-time Pharisee, to make. He once thought that keeping the Law was the way to life and that the gospel was actually leading people away from God. But he found out he was wrong. The Law was actually the agent ("through the Law") that showed him his sin and led him to the gospel. As a new creation in Christ, Paul "died" to the Law; that is, he stopped trying to please God by keeping the Law. He exchanged his damning pursuit of self-righteousness for the life-giving grace of Jesus Christ. He was a totally new person.

> "I have been crucified with Christ; and it is no longer I who live, but Christ lives in me; and the life which I now live in the flesh I live by faith in the Son of God, who loved me and gave Himself up for me." (v. 20)

What does Paul mean by his being "crucified with Christ"? He's alive, isn't he? He wasn't one of the thieves crucified on either side of Jesus on that dark day at Golgotha. Paul is using vivid figurative language here to communicate our union with Christ.

> Those who place their faith in Christ are united with him by that faith—united so closely that his experience now becomes theirs: they share his death to the old order ("under law"; cf. 4:4) and his

43

resurrection to new life. . . . As Christ's death was death by crucifixion, the believer is said not only to have died with him but to have been "crucified with him." . . . The figure is deliberately bold, designed to emphasize the finality of the death which has put an end to the old order and interposed a barrier between it and the new life in Christ. . . . The perfect tense . . . emphasizes that participation in the crucified Christ has become the believer's settled way of life.[4]

Before Christ, our only path to righteousness and pleasing God was through keeping the Law. Since, as sinners, we couldn't keep it, we stood condemned by the Law—deserving God's judgment. But when Jesus walked this earth, He obeyed His Father's Law perfectly. And when He died, He bore the Father's judgment for sinners.

When Jesus Christ died on the cross (literally), we also died (figuratively) to the old way of living, that is, trying to be righteous by keeping the Law or living in fear of its condemnation. Or, as Stott writes, "Being united to Christ in His sin-bearing death, my sinful past has been blotted out."[5] Stott goes on to explain how important it is that we grasp these truths in order to grow in the Christian life.

Perhaps now it is becoming clearer why a Christian who is "justified in Christ" is not free to sin. In Christ "old things are passed away" and "all things are become new" (2 Cor. 5:17, av). This is because the death and resurrection of Christ are not only historical events (He "gave himself" and now "lives"), but events in which through faith-union with Him His people have come to share ("I have been crucified with Christ" and now "I live"). Once we have been united to Christ in His death, our old life is finished; it is ridiculous to suggest that we could ever go back to it. Besides, we have risen to a new life. In one sense, we live this new life through faith in Christ. In another sense, it is not we who

4. Bruce, The Epistle to the Galatians, p. 144.
5. Stott, The Message of Galatians, p. 65.

live at all, but Christ lives it in us. And, living in us, He gives us new desires for holiness, for God, for heaven. It is not that we cannot sin again; we can. But we do not want to. The whole tenor of our life has changed. Everything is different now, because we ourselves are different. See how daringly personal Paul makes it: Christ "gave himself for *me*." "Christ . . . lives in *me*." No Christian who has grasped these truths could ever seriously contemplate reverting to the old life.[6]

Growing in Christ isn't about making ourselves new; it's about realizing that *we have been made new* in Christ Jesus; it's about living out who we are.

Unlike the Judaizers' message, Paul's gospel does not "nullify the grace of God" (v. 21a). By seeking to obtain righteousness by human effort, the Judaizers reject the grace of God. For if sinful people can obtain their own salvation through keeping the Law, then "Christ died needlessly" (v. 21b). His death was a waste; His precious blood was spilled in vain.

But it wasn't spilled in vain. His death was a purposeful, deliberate one, designed by God Himself to secure our salvation. So Christ could live in us. So we could live in Him . . . and for Him.

 Living Insights

"Who am I?"

When's the last time you really ruminated on that question? I'm not talking about what you do for a living or even what you like and dislike. But in the depths of your heart, in the silent recesses of your soul, who are you?

In case you're having a tough time answering, God has already answered for you. Take a look at the following passages that describe who we are as new creatures in Christ. After each one, write down your heartfelt response to God, or jot down a few implications of that passage for day-to-day living.

Romans 5:1–5 _____

---

6. Stott, *The Message of Galatians*, pp. 65–66.

2 Corinthians 5:17 _____

_____

_____

Galatians 2:20 _____

_____

_____

Ephesians 2:1–10 _____

_____

_____

Colossians 3:1–4_____

_____

_____

1 Peter 2:9–10_____

_____

_____

As believers in Jesus Christ, we are no longer God's enemies, but His friends. We have peace with Him. We are changed, and we are changing—becoming more like Him. We are God's beloved people, a "royal priesthood" raised up to show forth His glory. No longer dead spiritually, we are alive in Christ.

That's who we are. And we can know who we are because of who He is . . . and what He has done for us.

Chapter 7

BACKSLIDING INTO LEGALISM

Galatians 3:1–9

Nagano, Japan. In the 1998 Winter Olympic Games, athletes from around the world gathered there to put a lifetime of training on display for just a few minutes, a few seconds—hoping to feel the weight of a glittering medal around their necks and to bask in the glory of victory.

Years of sweat, pain, practice, competition, and saying no to lesser things brought them to that point. One television profile of a speed skater showed a home movie of the boy at five years old predicting, "I'm going to the Olympics when I grow up." And so he did.

But what if he or any other athlete, having finally arrived at the Olympics, had suddenly decided to walk away from the sport they had mastered and compete in an event for which they had never trained? What if a figure skater favored to win the gold decided to try her luck at the luge instead? What if a bobsledder who always wanted to play hockey turned in his spandex, suited up in pads, grabbed a stick, and skated onto the ice (or tried to)? And what about those curlers (curling is that strange sport that looks like shuffleboard on ice)? Could you imagine one of them entering the ski jump competition?

We would have one response to such last-minute changes: "Are you nuts? You've come so far! How could you throw it all away? How could you turn your back on the sport that has brought you here? How foolish!"

How foolish indeed. But not nearly as foolish as turning your back on the grace that saved you and instead embracing a legalistic way of living—which brings only condemnation. That's what the Galatians did, and that's why Paul called them "foolish."

A Strong Rebuke

Having established that his gospel is God's gospel (chaps. 1 and 2), Paul again turns to the Galatians' spiritual defection in chapter 3. Using strong language, he shows that living under the Law and living under grace are mutually exclusive lifestyles.

> You foolish Galatians, who has bewitched you, before whose eyes Jesus Christ was publicly portrayed as crucified? (3:1)

The Greek word for *foolish* denotes mindless behavior, acting without thinking. The J. B. Phillips translation is even more blunt:

> O you dear idiots of Galatia, who saw Jesus Christ the crucified so plainly, who has been casting a spell over you?

So irrational is the Galatians' abandonment of grace that it appears they have been "bewitched," led astray by sorcery. The Judaizers had, in a sense, mesmerized them into thinking they could earn God's favor by keeping the Law. This powerful charm of legalism[1] pulled the Galatians away from Christ, whose crucifixion Paul had placarded[2] before them and in whom they had already placed their trust. "Paul had vividly and graphically proclaimed the crucified Christ to the Galatians; yet their eyes had been diverted from the Cross to the Law."[3]

A Series of Questions

After rebuking the Galatians, Paul now asks them a series of four rhetorical questions designed to reveal the foolishness of trying to live under the Law.

The Question of Receiving the Spirit

> This is the only thing I want to find out from you: did you receive the Spirit by the works of the Law, or by hearing with faith? (v. 2)

1. In an enlightening discussion of legalism, Charles C. Ryrie offers this definition of the term: "Legalism may be defined as 'a fleshly attitude which conforms to a code for the purpose of exalting self.'" *Balancing the Christian Life* (Chicago, Ill.: Moody Bible Institute of Chicago, 1994), p. 168.

2. William Barclay translates the phrase "publicly portrayed" as "placarded." He writes, "It is the Greek word *(prographein)* that would be used for putting up a poster. It is actually used for a notice put up by a father to say that he will no longer be responsible for his son's debts; it is also used for putting up the announcement of an auction sale." *The Letters to the Galatians and Ephesians*, rev. ed., The Daily Study Bible Series (Philadelphia, Pa.: Westminster Press, 1976), pp. 24–25.

3. Donald K. Campbell, "Galatians," in *The Bible Knowledge Commentary*, New Testament edition, ed. John F. Walvoord and Roy B. Zuck (Colorado Springs, Colo.: Chariot Victor Publishing, 1983), p. 596.

The Galatians knew they had received the Holy Spirit upon believing Paul's gospel and putting their trust in Jesus Christ. The Spirit didn't come to indwell them as some kind of reward for living up to the Law's demands; He was given to them as God's gift.

The Question of Living by the Spirit

The Spirit, however, doesn't indwell us and then leave us to live on our own.

> Are you so foolish? Having begun by the Spirit, are
> you now being perfected by the flesh? (v. 3)

Paul's point is this: The Spirit came to indwell you by faith. Now He is causing you to progress in the Christian life. Why would you try to live your new Spirit-life in the power of your old works-life?

Remember, Paul is talking to Christians—people who are already saved. So legalism's distortion of the gospel doesn't just keep people from being saved, it keeps saved people from growing in their faith. Legalism hinders both justification (God's declaring the sinner righteous through faith in Christ) and sanctification (the process of growing in Christ).

We are saved by faith, and we live the Christian life by faith. To embrace Christ by faith and then resort to living by works is inconsistent and incomprehensible.

The Question of Suffering

And what about the suffering the Galatians had endured for the sake of the gospel? If they turned now to works, all that suffering would have been in vain.

> Did you suffer so many things in vain—if indeed it
> was in vain? (v. 4)

Living the Christian life was no piece of cake; both Paul and the Galatians knew that. The Galatians had, no doubt, experienced their share of ostracism and persecution for their faith. Their fellow Gentiles who still worshiped idols would have scoffed at the idea of one God—and an invisible one at that. And some of the Jews, as we have already seen, accused the grace-exalting Galatians of impugning the Law.

Yet the Galatians endured all that because they believed Paul's message of grace. If they put themselves back under the Law, that suffering would mean nothing.

49

The Question of Miracles

Just one more question, Galatians:

> So then, does He who provides you with the Spirit
> and works miracles among you, do it by the works
> of the Law, or by hearing with faith? (v. 5)

Commentators differ on exactly what Paul is asking here. Because of the close association between the Spirit and miracles, some commentators believe Paul is talking about the Galatians' spiritual gifts, particularly those involving the miraculous manifestations of God's power. Paul's argument, then, would be that trying to keep the Law doesn't enable a person to perform miracles. Rather, those gifts come by way of faith and are given when a person believes the gospel.

Others interpret these miracles to be displays of power that Paul performed before the Galatians when he was among them (see Acts 14:3, 8–11). These, though not necessarily caused by the Galatians' faith, were put on display to lead them to faith in Christ.

Still others believe that Paul isn't limiting "miracles" to outward displays of supernatural power but is including the inward miracle of salvation.

Whether Paul had all of these ideas in mind or just one of them, we don't know for sure. But we can be certain about this: none of them came by works. They were all phenomena of faith.

Systematically, question by question, like a prosecuting attorney whittling down a witness, Paul exposes the futility of legalism. Did you receive the Spirit by works of the Law? No. Do you progress in the Christian life by depending on your own works? Of course not. Did you suffer for the sake of works? Nope. And how about the miracles displayed in your midst? Did they come by keeping the Law? No again.

"Your whole life in Christ revolves around faith," Paul seems to be saying. "Why in the world would you go back to trying to keep the Law? Move forward in freedom instead of backward toward bondage!"

The Faith of Abraham

The Judaizers, however, had so strongly emphasized Moses as the preeminent Jew and the Mosaic Law as the model for religion that Paul's argument may still not have convinced the Galatians to turn back to grace. So Paul went even further back in Jewish history, before Moses, to Abraham, and showed that the very father of the Jewish nation was saved by faith and not by keeping the Law.

> Even so Abraham believed God, and it was reckoned to him as righteousness. (Gal. 3:6)

Paul is quoting Genesis 15:6, where Abraham responded to God's promise of an heir and countless descendants. Abraham— old and childless—believed that God would do as He promised. And God "reckoned it to him as righteousness." This first Jew was justified—not by keeping the Law—but by faith! More than a decade passed before God instituted circumcision (see Gen. 17), and the Mosaic Law wouldn't arrive until some four hundred years later.

Then Paul goes on to explain that the Galatians themselves, and all believers—Jews and Gentiles alike—are the spiritual descendants of Abraham.

> Therefore, be sure that it is those who are of faith who are sons of Abraham. The Scripture, foreseeing that God would justify the Gentiles by faith, preached the gospel beforehand to Abraham, saying, "All the nations will be blessed in you." So then those who are of faith are blessed with Abraham, the believer. (Gal. 3:7–9)

"So, you Galatians want a little Jewishness in your Christianity? You already have it. You, and all people who come to Christ by faith, are the spiritual descendants of Abraham, the father of the Jews. You don't have to be a Pharisee, a Judaizer, or any other brand of legalist to be part of God's people. You just have to believe in Christ by faith." That is the gist of Paul's case.

Luging won't help a skater win the gold. And legalism won't help a Christian grow. It does just the opposite. It hinders maturity. It suffocates freedom. It obscures the grace of God. Stay with what brought you this far. Stay with grace.

 Living Insights

In the Christian life, looking back is sometimes as important to our growth as looking ahead. Sometimes it's our recollection of when "Jesus Christ was publicly portrayed as crucified" before us that keeps us from slipping into legalism.

Do you remember when you first embraced the gospel? When your condition as a sinner separated from God became clear? Do you recall when you first understood that Jesus Christ suffered the punishment God had stored up for you and transferred His own righteousness to your account? Do you remember when it clicked that you couldn't work your way to God, so you put your faith in the perfect life, atoning death, and glorious resurrection of Jesus?

Perhaps you can't pinpoint the exact moment of your conversion. You may have grown up with Christian parents who started reading the Bible to you before you could even talk. And as soon as you could talk, one of the first things you learned was a creed or catechism or passage of Scripture. Yet you can say without hesitation that you believe the gospel and have put your complete trust in Jesus Christ for your salvation.

Whatever your background, take some time to get your core beliefs down on paper. And when the lure of legalism dangles before your heart, come back to this page—and feed instead on the grace of God.

The truth about me when I was a sinner separated from God (Rom. 3:9–18; 1 Cor. 6:9–10; Eph. 2:1–3):

_____

_____

_____

The truth about Jesus Christ, not human works, being the only way back to God (John 14:6; Acts 4:12; Col. 1:21–23):

_____

_____

_____

The truth about the life I now live by faith in Christ (Matt. 28:20b; Rom. 6:1–11, 22; 8:1–4; 1 Cor. 6:11; Eph. 2:10; 1 Pet. 2:1–3):

_____

_____

_____

Chapter 8

DELIVERED FROM
A CURSE
Galatians 3:10–14

What does it take to get into heaven?

It takes a perfect life. Flawless obedience to God. Loving Him with every fiber of our being and loving others as ourselves. Every thought, every motive, every action must be pure, holy, untainted by sin.

Wait a minute! Haven't we been talking about grace throughout this study? Haven't we learned that imperfect people—sinners—are made right with God through Jesus Christ and bound for heaven?

Yes, but it still takes perfection to get into heaven. As Paul explains in these next verses, such a perfect life must be lived either *by* us or *for* us. And since no one but Jesus Christ has ever lived a perfect life, He is the only One who can grant that perfect life to sinners.

The Cursed Life of the Law

Drawing upon the Galatians' salvation experience and the justification of Abraham, Paul has shown that a life saved by faith continues to mature by faith (3:1–9). Beginning in verse 10, the apostle continues to champion the life of faith by explaining that the Law, rather than adding anything to salvation, actually nullifies it. Because those who try to live by the Law are under a curse.

"Cursed Is Everyone"

> For as many as are of the works of the Law are under a curse; for it is written, "Cursed is everyone who does not abide by all things written in the book of the Law, to perform them." (v. 10)

What is Paul saying here? First, who are "as many as are of the works of the Law"? They are all those who, like the Judaizers, assume they can keep the Law, thus pleasing God and earning salvation for themselves.

53

But keeping the Law, as Paul points out next, means keeping the *entire* Law. He quotes Deuteronomy 27:26, the words Moses spoke to the Israelites prior to their entering the Promised Land. Moses reminded the people that partial obedience is disobedience. They must obey God *fully*. If they were to break *any* of His laws, they would be "cursed"—condemned, judged, rejected—by Him, because that is the condition of the Law.

Paul's point, then, is that all people—Jews, Gentiles, everyone—who fail to keep the Law in its entirety live under the shadow of God's impending judgment (see also James 2:10).

How different from what the Judaizers, and the Galatians influenced by them, were thinking. They thought their pursuit of the Law was earning God's favor, but it was actually arousing His judgment.

Since the Law does not justify, how then can we be made right with God?

The Righteous Shall Live by Faith

> Now that no one is justified by the Law before God is evident; for, "The righteous man shall live by faith." (Gal. 3:11)

Paul draws upon the prophet Habakkuk's record of the Lord's words to him:

> "Behold, as for the proud one,
> His soul is not right within him;
> But the righteous will live by his faith."
> (Hab. 2:4)

God had just revealed to Habakkuk that the southern kingdom of Judah was going to fall to the Babylonians (probably collectively referred to as "the proud one" in the first line). Habakkuk was initially stunned, but God reassured him that Babylon itself would not go unpunished. That cruel kingdom would triumph for a time by its strength, but God would have the ultimate triumph. And His people, those who trusted in Him no matter how bleak the circumstances, would be delivered by their sovereign God.

Paul's use of Habakkuk shows that "the same principle that was applicable in the realm of national deliverance is applicable in the area of spiritual deliverance (salvation)."[1] Eternal life comes not to

---

1. Robert Mounce, note on Habakkuk 2:4, in *The NIV Study Bible*, ed. Kenneth L. Barker and others (Grand Rapids, Mich.: Zondervan Bible Publishers, 1985), p. 1389.

the "proud," those seeking salvation by keeping the Law, but to the humble, those who recognize their need for a righteous substitute and put their trust in Christ.

Law and Faith Are Mutually Exclusive for Salvation

You can almost hear the Galatians responding, "OK, Paul. You've made your point. Salvation is by faith in Christ. But can't the Law be at least part of the equation? What's wrong with mixing a little Law in with faith? After all, the Law came from God too, just like the gospel."

Paul, though, makes it very clear that faith and the Law cannot blend to accomplish salvation.

> However, the Law is not of faith; on the contrary, "He who practices them shall live by them." (Gal. 3:12)

Commentator Leon Morris elaborates on this incompatibility of law and faith.

> [Paul] insists that justification before God is the result of trusting God, not of achieving merit by one's own efforts. . . . What he is insisting "is that faith and the observance of Law are incompatible as grounds of *justification*." The law is concerned with doing things; it prescribes conduct. But faith is not concerned with doing things; it means trusting someone. And because Scripture speaks of faith as the way to God, salvation cannot be by works. . . . Doing something to merit salvation is one thing; trusting God to do what is needed is quite another.[2]

Does that mean that good works have no place in the Christian life? Not at all. Good works are the outgrowth of new life in Christ (see Rom 6:1–7, 11–14; Eph. 2:10; James 1:22). But as far as justification is concerned, faith in Christ apart from works is the only way to God.

---

2. Leon Morris, *Galatians: Paul's Charter of Christian Freedom* (Downers Grove, Ill.: Inter-Varsity Press, 1996), p. 105. Morris quotes George Duncan, *The Epistle of Paul to the Galatians* (London, 1934).

The Blessed Life of Faith

How does faith remove us from under the Law's curse? It happens like this: Someone else had to suffer the curse for us. Someone else had to jump in front of us and "take the bullet" of God's judgment. That someone else was Jesus Christ.

Jesus Bore the Curse, So We Wouldn't Have To

> Christ redeemed us from the curse of the Law, having become a curse for us—for it is written, "Cursed is everyone who hangs on a tree." (Gal. 3:13)

The Greek word for *redeemed* means "to buy out of slavery." Jesus snatched us out of the enslaving curse of the Law; He rescued us from God's judgment against sin. How? He became a curse for us.

> This is a strong declaration of substitutionary redemption whereby Christ took the penalty of all guilty lawbreakers on Himself. Thus the "curse of the Law" was transferred from sinners to Christ, the sinless One (cf. 1 Peter 3:18), and He delivered people from it. The confirming quotation from Deuteronomy 21:23 refers to the fact that in Old Testament times criminals were executed (normally by stoning) and then displayed on a stake or post to show God's divine rejection. When Christ was crucified, it was evidence He had come under the curse of God. The manner of His death was a great obstacle to faith for Jews until they realized the curse He bore was for them (cf. Isa. 53).[3]

That's grace. The eternal Son of God—sinless, glorious, holy—slipped out of His perfect heaven and into a sin-infested world. He voluntarily took what we deserved, the judgment of God against sin, and gave us what we could never earn, righteous standing before God.

Why? Paul closes this section with two reasons: (1) that all who believe might receive the blessing of salvation promised to Abraham (Gal. 3:14a), and (2) that we would receive the Holy Spirit (v. 14b).

---

3. Donald K. Campbell, "Galatians," in *The Bible Knowledge Commentary*, New Testament edition, ed. John F. Walvoord and Roy B. Zuck (Colorado Springs, Colo.: Chariot Victor Publishing, 1983), p. 598.

By faith, we have become part of Abraham's family of faith; we have been swept up into God's eternal plan of redemption. And by faith, God's Spirit now indwells us. The Spirit is the assurance of our intimate union with Jesus Christ and the promise that we will one day see Him face-to-face.

Yes, it takes perfection to get into heaven—Jesus' perfection. It takes the life He lived obediently under the Law and sacrificed willingly on the cross. These alone will save us from judgment and bring us back to God.

"Faith," says John R. W. Stott, "is laying hold of Jesus Christ personally. There is no merit in it. It is not another 'work.' Its value is not in itself, but entirely in its object, Jesus Christ."[4]

That's true for entering the Christian life . . . and for living it.

 Living Insights

Faith in Christ is required to enter the Christian life. It is also essential in living it. Just as it's not our own righteousness that saves us, it's not our own righteousness that matures us. Trying to live the Christian life on our own is as foolish as trying to save ourselves.

That's not to say we should sit back and do nothing and expect to grow. We make choices and plans. We actively pursue what is good and right. We exercise self-discipline, and so on. But our strength for living comes from Christ. We are "in Him." That means we make choices and plans according to His wisdom, guided by His Word. It also means that He gets the credit for all our spiritual successes—the blessings we receive, the change in our hearts, the people we lead to Christ. He who began a good work in us, as Paul said, will perfect that work (Phil. 1:6).

Sometimes, though, we don't feel as though Jesus is at work in us at all. We feel disconnected from Him. We feel as though it's "up to me" now. So we depend on ourselves more than Him. We panic instead of pray. We delude ourselves into thinking that we should carry all the burdens for our family, our friends, our church, the world.

4. Reprinted from *The Message of Galatians* (BST) by John R. W. Stott. © 1968 by John R. W. Stott. Used by permission from InterVarsity Press, P. O. Box 1400, Downers Grove, Ill. 60515, p. 82.

Does that strike a familiar chord with you? Is there any area of life that you seem to be living more by your own effort than by faith in Christ? Jot it down.

_____

_____

_____

_____

_____

What do Paul's words to the Galatians about Jesus' desire and power to save tell you about His desire and power to help you in this situation?

_____

_____

_____

_____

He can be trusted to save us . . . and sustain us.

Chapter 9

A Promise You Can Count On

Galatians 3:15–22

Do you keep your promises?

Once you give your word, how long does it stand? Suppose you promise your four-year-old that you'll take him to Disneyland for his fifth birthday, which happens to be six months away. There it is. Locked in. An unconditional promise. Come rain or shine, crowded or not, regardless of your work schedule or the child's behavior between now and then—you're going to see Mickey. Mark it in red on the calendar.

About three months pass, however, and your son starts exhibiting some challenging behavioral problems—you know, the kind that make you wonder what you were thinking when you decided to have kids. Part of your plan to correct the behavior involves rewarding obedience and reproving disobedience.

You don't bribe and threaten, mind you; you genuinely want to encourage responsible behavior and get to the heart of your child. Perhaps you end a particularly good day by going out for ice cream and heaping words of praise and encouragement on your son. Or maybe you decide to temporarily withhold privileges, like television, for rebellious behavior.

Your plan seems to be working; the little guy actually seems to enjoy doing the right thing. Then, the evening before the Disneyland trip, he responds to your instructions to clean up his room by throwing the mother of all temper tantrums.

"Disneyland? Ha!" you say to yourself. "Mickey and Goofy will be in an old cartoon character's home by the time my kid gets to go there."

But guess what? You promised him Disneyland on his birthday. Period. Are you going to let the boy's failure to obey deprive him of the unconditional promise you made six months ago? You could end up punishing his aberrant behavior while relinquishing the integrity of your word.

Unfortunately, we don't always make the right decision in such situations. But God always does; He always keeps His promises to His children. Nothing, not even our disobedience, can invalidate His promise to save us through faith in Jesus Christ. Though we fail to keep His Law, God never fails to keep His word. This timeless trustworthiness of God's promise, as Paul explains in our next passage, is yet another reason for the Galatians to reject the Judaizers' claim that keeping the Law must be part of salvation.

Paul's Ongoing Argument for Faith

Thus far in his letter, Paul's message to the Galatians has been unrelenting: "A man is not justified by the works of the Law but through faith in Christ Jesus" (2:16a).

He has called the Judaizers "accursed" (1:8–9). He has shown that his gospel came directly from Jesus Christ and matches the message preached by the other apostles (1:11–2:10). Paul even confronted Peter in Antioch when Peter's legalistic behavior obscured the gospel (2:11–14).

How, Paul wondered, could the Galatians abandon the very message that gave them life (3:1–5)? Not even Abraham, the father of the Jews, was justified by the Law but by faith (vv. 6–9). How could the Galatians expect to please God according to the Law, which condemns rather than justifies? It is by faith in Christ, who bore the curse of the Law for us, accepting our deserved judgment, that we receive the blessing of eternal life (vv. 10–14).

Who could argue with that? The Judaizers, of course.

Abraham and Moses: The Context of 3:15–22

You can almost hear the Judaizers' response: "OK, maybe Abraham *was* justified by faith. But that was before the Mosaic Law was given at Sinai. Once the Law came, *it* became the vehicle for salvation and superseded everything that came before it."

Also, with Paul's hammering so hard on the Law's inability to save sinners, perhaps the Galatians began to wonder if he saw any value or goodness in the Law at all.

Undoubtedly anticipating these questions, Paul turns his discussion to the relationship between the gospel promised to Abraham and the Law given to Moses.

Paul began teaching from Abraham's life in 3:6. In 3:15, though, he wants to do more than focus on the patriarch's salvation experience. He wants to show that Abraham's justification—and, in fact, the salvation of every believer—was and is based on God's covenant, His eternal plan to impart salvation to sinners. The Mosaic Law, though coming centuries after Abraham, didn't change that plan. On the contrary, the Law was *part of* the plan; it was intended to drive us to God's gracious promise and into the fold of the covenant community.

The Law Does Not Replace the Promise

The first half of this passage, verses 15–18, is primarily negative, emphasizing what the Law could not accomplish. Verses 19–22 are positive, explaining the purpose of the Law.

The Permanence of Covenants

In order to explain the superiority of the gospel over the Law, Paul frames his argument in language the Galatians would understand ("in terms of human relations," v. 15a). He says,

> Even though it is only a man's covenant, yet when it has been ratified, no one sets it aside or adds conditions to it. (v. 15b)

This is Paul's first use of the term *covenant* (in the Greek, *diathēkē*) in the letter. The term has several nuances. In its formal, Old Testament sense, the Hebrew term *berith* "applied to various transactions between God and man, and man and his fellowman."[1] A covenant could be between two individuals, tribes, or nations. It could involve two equal parties or a greater party and lesser party (such as a conquering king and a vassal king).

A covenant held both parties to certain obligations and specified penalties for breaching the pact. Covenants were often sealed with a solemn ceremony, such as the slaughtering and dissecting of animals—a gruesome picture of what would happen if either party broke the covenant (see Gen. 15:9–10, 17).

---

1. Merrill F. Unger, *The New Unger's Bible Dictionary*, revised and updated edition, ed. R. K. Harrison, Howard F. Vos, and Cyril J. Barber (Chicago, Ill.: Moody Press, 1988), p. 259.

God deals with His people within a covenantal framework.[2] In His covenant with Noah, God promised never to destroy the world by flood again (Gen. 9:8–17). God covenanted with Abraham to make his descendants more numerous than the stars, to give him the Promised Land, and to bless all nations through him (Gen. 12:1–3; chap. 15). At Mount Sinai, under Moses' leadership, the Israelites promised to obey God's Law, thus agreeing to the covenantal terms He had stipulated (Exod. 24:3; see also chaps. 19–24). God's covenant with David expanded on the Abrahamic covenant, specifying that the promise made to Abraham—Christ Himself—would come through the royal line of David (2 Sam. 7:12, 16; 22:51). And Jesus Christ, the Mediator of the "new covenant," offered Himself as the true and final sacrifice for sin (Luke 22:20).

In the Greek culture, though, *diathēkē* was also used for a will or testament. Commentators vary on how Paul meant to use the term here in Galatians 3. It could be that he began in verse 15 with the Galatians' understanding of the term—that of a will—but expanded it to include the formal Old Testament sense as he argued from the life of Abraham (v. 17).

Whatever the exact nuance of the term here in Galatians, Paul's point is clear: Binding agreements, be they formal covenants or legal wills, are unalterable. And if that's true in human relationships, how much more when God draws up the document—like the covenant He made with Abraham.

The Promise of a "Seed"

In verse 16, Paul moves from the general illustration of a human covenant to the specific promise contained in God's covenant with Abraham:

> Now the promises were spoken to Abraham and to his seed. He does not say, "And to seeds," as referring to many, but rather to one, "And to your seed," that is, Christ.

---

2. God's covenants with people are often designated as "conditional" or "unconditional." His promise to Noah not to destroy the world by water again was unconditional—God didn't require anything of Noah for that promise to be kept. In contrast, the Mosaic Law was conditional—Israel was obligated to keep the Law to receive God's blessing. The Abrahamic covenant was both unconditional and conditional. God's choosing to bless Abraham and his descendants wasn't predicated on anything Abraham did, but Abraham's faith relationship to God obligated the patriarch to trust and obey Him in all things.

Paul is explaining to the Galatians how they, through their faith in Christ, have been incorporated into the promises God made to Abraham. John R. W. Stott elaborates.

God promised an inheritance to Abraham and his posterity. Paul knew perfectly well that the immediate, literal reference of this promise was to the land of Canaan, which God was going to give to Abraham's physical descendants. But he also knew that this did not exhaust its meaning; nor was it the ultimate reference in God's mind. Indeed, it could not have been, for God said that in Abraham's seed all the families of the earth would be blessed, and how could the whole world be blessed through Jews living in the land of Canaan? Paul realized that both the "land" which was promised and the "seed" to whom it was promised were ultimately spiritual. God's purpose was not just to give the land of Canaan to the Jews, but to give salvation (a spiritual inheritance) to believers who are in Christ. Further, Paul argues, this truth was implicit in the word God used, which was not the plural "children" or "descendants," but the singular "seed" or "posterity," a collective noun referring to Christ and to all those who are in Christ by faith (verse 16).

Such was God's promise. It was free and unconditional. As we might say, there were "no strings attached." There were no works to do, no laws to obey, no merit to establish, no conditions to fulfil. God simply said, "I will give you a seed. To your seed I will give the land, and in your seed all the nations of the earth will be blessed." His promise was like a will, freely giving the inheritance to a future generation. And like a human will, this divine promise is unalterable. It is still in force today, for it has never been rescinded. God does not make promises in order to break them. He has never annulled or modified His will.[3]

3. Reprinted from *The Message of Galatians* (BST) by John R. W. Stott. © 1968 by John R. W. Stott. Used by permission from InterVarsity Press, P. O. Box 1400, Downers Grove, Ill. 60515, pp. 88–89.

Wow! Did you realize that, as a believer in Jesus Christ, you are a spiritual descendant of Abraham? You are part of the fulfillment of God's covenant to the patriarch. And that means, as Paul has been arguing, that it's the promise—not the Law—that makes you part of God's family.

Still Valid after 430 Years

And when God makes a promise, it stands for all time.

> What I am saying is this: the Law, which came four hundred and thirty years later, does not invalidate a covenant previously ratified by God, so as to nullify the promise. For if the inheritance is based on law, it is no longer based on a promise; but God has granted it to Abraham by means of a promise. (vv. 17–18)

Though 430 years[4] had elapsed between the Abrahamic covenant and the Mosaic Law, the latter did not supersede the former. Even before Abraham (in eternity past, as a matter of fact; see Eph. 1:3–6), God decided to call a people to Himself and give them the gift of eternal life. He accomplished this through the meritorious life and sacrificial death of His Son. Faith in Jesus Christ, not our vain attempts to keep the Law, is what saves us. Keeping the Law and trusting by faith are mutually exclusive in terms of salvation. You can't have salvation based on the Law *and* the gospel. Neither can you have it by the Law alone. Faith in Christ, and that alone, will render sinners acceptable to almighty God.

The Law Prepares Us for the Promise

Is Paul impugning the Law? Is he saying that it was unnecessary or that God should have never given it? These were, no doubt, the accusations the Judaizers were hurling at him. But there's no way

---

4. Commentators differ as to the exact period designated by the 430 years. Some scholars, citing Exodus 12:40, which gives that duration as the number of years the Hebrews spent in Egyptian slavery, say that Paul was designating the transitional period between the age of promise (whose final figure was Joseph) and the age of Law (instituted by Moses). Others believe the 430 years designates the time that elapsed between God's confirmation of the Abrahamic covenant to Jacob and the giving of the Law. Whatever the exact period, Paul's point is clear: Neither the passing of time nor the giving of the Law has rescinded God's promise to Abraham.

those accusations could stick, for Paul clearly explains that the Law has a purpose.

The Law Was Added "Because of Transgressions"

> It was added because of transgressions, having been ordained through angels by the agency of a mediator, until the seed would come to whom the promise had been made. Now a mediator is not for one party only; whereas God is only one. (vv. 19–20)

"Because of transgressions." There's the purpose of the Law. As one writer put it, "Satan would have us to prove ourselves holy by the law, which God gave to prove us sinners."[5] God wanted to provide His people with a clear statement of His standards, with unequivocal definitions of righteousness and sin—so that when they failed to meet His perfect requirements, they would seek His grace (see also Rom. 3:19–20; 5:20–21). The Law, then, looked ahead to the "seed who would come," the Person through whom transgression of the Law would be forgiven.

Paul's reference to angels emphasizes that these heavenly beings were somehow involved in the giving of the Law at Sinai along with the "mediator," who was Moses (Exod. 23:20–23; 20:18–21). Other passages also mention the involvement of angels in the giving of the Law (Deut. 33:2; Acts 7:53; Heb. 2:2). This is yet another reason why Paul's opponents couldn't accuse him of denigrating the Law. He openly acknowledges that it was given, not only through Moses, the great servant of God, but through angels. The Law is heavenly in its origin; therefore, it is holy and good.

Galatians 3:20 is enigmatic, generating some three hundred interpretations. Paul seems to be once again emphasizing the priority of the promise over the Law. The Law involved God's giving it and the people's obligation to follow it—two parties were involved ("for one party only"). However, the promise, fulfilled in the gospel, is unilateral ("God is one"), meaning that God not only gave the Law but keeps all its conditions on our behalf through the meritorious work of Christ.

The Law Is Not Contrary to the Promises of God

Paul has shown the purpose of the Law in God's plan. But the

---

5. Andrew Jukes, as quoted by Stott in *The Message of Galatians*, p. 90.

Judaizers probably still objected, accusing Paul of teaching "that the law becomes evil because it is in opposition to grace as the true means of salvation."[6] Is that what Paul is doing? Is he somehow making God out to be inconsistent or in conflict with Himself? Here's his response:

> Is the Law then contrary to the promises of God? May it never be! For if a law had been given which was able to impart life, then righteousness would indeed have been based on law. But the Scripture has shut up everyone under sin, so that the promise by faith in Jesus Christ might be given to those who believe. (vv. 21–22)

The Law and the gospel are both part of God's plan. The Law shows us our sin, and the gospel shows us the way to escape from sin's penalty and hold on our life. In that sense, the Law and the gospel are complementary, not contradictory. If the Law could "impart life," God would really be inconsistent. That would mean He had two plans for salvation—one by human performance and one by faith in Christ.

But God has only one plan for salvation: that sinners, having been shown by the Law that they are "shut up under sin," would by faith flee to Jesus Christ, our only hope for eternal life. Martin Luther put it this way:

> The principal point . . . of the law . . . is to make men not better but worse; that is to say, it sheweth unto them their sin, that by the knowledge thereof they may be humbled, terrified, bruised and broken, and by this means may be driven to seek grace, and so to come to that blessed Seed (sc. Christ).[7]

If you have put your faith in Christ, you are loved by God, you're a member of His family, you are free from the condemnation of the Law. That's a promise that will never be broken.

---

6. Taken from *The Expositor's Bible Commentary*, volume 10, edited by Frank E. Gaebelein. Copyright © 1976 by The Zondervan Corporation. Used by permission of Zondervan Publishing House, p. 465.

7. Martin Luther, as quoted by Stott in *The Message of Galatians*, p. 91.

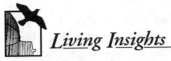 *Living Insights*

Is it really all that hard to keep God's Law? If we really concentrate, if we really focus, we should be able to, right? Let's take a couple of the Ten Commandments and see.

"You shall not murder." No problem there. Many of us have hunted birds and squirrels, but that's not what God had in mind here.

How about "You shall not commit adultery"? What's that you say? You've been married to the same spouse for thirty years and have never been unfaithful? In fact, your marriage is stronger than ever? That's wonderful!

Let's consider, though, what Jesus said it takes to keep these commandments perfectly. Thumb over to Matthew 5 and take just a few minutes to read verses 21–22 and 27–28. What is Jesus saying about the Law? Is keeping it just a matter of outward conformity, or does it require absolute purity of thought, motives, etc.?

_____

_____

_____

Now flip over to Exodus 20 and read the Ten Commandments as listed in verses 1–17. Using Jesus' explanation of keeping the commandments, how many do you think you've kept? All of them? Most of them? None of them?

_____

Let's be honest; we've broken them all. We've kept none of them perfectly. None of us is without idols; we've all put other people, possessions, priorities ahead of God. We've all lied. Out of discontentment, we've all wanted something someone else had. And those are just the ones we can remember! Imagine all the times we sin in thought and deed and don't even know we're doing it.

We can't keep the Law. But praise be to God that someone kept it for us. Jesus Christ never sinned. His every thought, motive, and action complied with God's Law. He always honored his earthly parents. He never put anything ahead of His Heavenly Father. He kept the Sabbath without fail. He never, ever lied.

Jesus earned for us the righteous life that sin keeps us from attaining. Clothed in His perfection, we appear as perfect Law-keepers before the Great Judge. When God looks at us, He sees the flawless obedience of His Son . . . and accepts us.

And, because we are in Christ, the Law never has the last word. Though our performance under the Law fails, the promise of God never does.

Chapter 10

FROM LAW TO FAITH: OUR NEW STATUS IN CHRIST

Galatians 3:23–29

In this closing section of chapter 3, Paul continues to explain why God gave us the Law. But, as commentator James Montgomery Boice explains, these verses also contain something new.

> Before, [Paul] has been concerned with the law's true purpose, which is to lead men to Christ. Now, though he begins with this point, he soon moves on to the idea of a change of status for those who have passed from being under the bondage of the law to being sons in Christ. Before, we were prisoners, shut up under the law as under a guardian. Now we are sons, being reconciled to God and being made one with one another and with all who throughout history have been justified on the basis of God's promise.[1]

Sometimes we forget that the grace of God did more than just rescue us from bondage; it brought us into God's family. That's the way God works. He adopts whomever He rescues. Remember the Israelites under Egyptian bondage? God didn't free them so they could run around on their own; He freed them so they could be *His own.* He said to Moses,

> "Say, therefore, to the sons of Israel, 'I am the Lord, and I will bring you out from under the burdens of the Egyptians, and I will deliver you from their bondage. I will also redeem you with an outstretched arm and with great judgments. Then I will take you for My people, and I will be your God; and you shall know that I am the Lord your God, who brought you out from under the burdens of the Egyptians.'" (Exod. 6:6–7)

---

1. Taken from *The Expositor's Bible Commentary*, volume 10, edited by Frank E. Gaebelein. Copyright © 1976 by The Zondervan Corporation. Used by permission of Zondervan Publishing House, p. 467.

The same is true with all who have put their faith in Jesus Christ. We're free from the bondage of all our old masters—sin, legalism, the fear of God's judgment. That, however, is not the end of the story. We have a whole new identity, an entirely new orientation. We're now sons and daughters of the Most High God. And, as Paul explains, the Law was part of God's plan to bring us to this point.

Before Christ: Imprisoned and Tutored by the Law

We can look at Galatians 3:23–29 as a "before and after" story. To help us understand who we are, Paul reminds us where we came from. In verses 23–24, he uses vivid imagery to communicate the Law's role in bringing us to faith. Then, in verses 25–29, he describes our present position in Christ.

Locked Up by the Law

Before we trusted in Christ, says Paul, we were

> kept in custody under the law, being shut up to the faith which was later to be revealed. (v. 23)

The Greek word for "kept in custody," John R. W. Stott explains,

> means to "protect by military guards." . . . When applied to a city, it was used both of keeping the enemy out and of keeping the inhabitants in, lest they should flee or desert.[2]

To be "shut up" (vv. 22, 23) is a similar term, meaning to "'hem in' or 'coop up.'"[3] Before we exercised faith in Christ, we were imprisoned by the Law. As *The NIV Study Bible* points out, "To be a prisoner of sin (v. 22) and a prisoner of law amounts to much the same, because law reveals and stimulates sin (see 4:3; Ro 7:8; Col 2:20)."[4]

So there we were, behind the bars of the Law, powerless to do anything but sin—until faith came, which was "revealed" in Jesus

2. Reprinted from *The Message of Galatians* (BST) by John R. W. Stott. © 1968 by John R. W. Stott. Used by permission from InterVarsity Press, P. O. Box 1400, Downers Grove, Ill. 60515, p. 96.

3. Stott, *The Message of Galatians*, p. 96.

4. Robert Mounce, note on Galatians 3:23, in *The NIV Study Bible*, ed. Kenneth L. Barker and others (Grand Rapids, Mich.: Zondervan Bible Publishers, 1985), p. 1784.

Christ.[5] But the Law did more than imprison us. It also disciplined us.

A Harsh Disciplinarian

Paul also says the Law served as "our tutor to lead us to Christ, so that we may be justified by faith" (Gal. 3:24). We usually think of a tutor as a freelance teacher, but that image doesn't do the Greek word justice. James Montgomery Boice paints a more complete picture for us.

> The term [for "tutor"] is *paidagōgos*, which means "a child-custodian" or "child-attendant." The pedagogue was a slave employed by wealthy Greeks or Romans to have responsibility for one of the children of the family. He had charge of the child from about the years six to sixteen and was responsible for watching over his behavior wherever he went and for conducting him to and from school. The pedagogue did not teach. Therefore the translation "schoolmaster" [in the King James Version] is wrong; if Paul had meant this, he would have used *didaskalos* rather than *paidagōgos*. Paul's point is that this responsibility ceased when the child entered into the fullness of his position as a son, becoming an acknowledged adult by the formal rite of adoption by his father.[6]

Stott adds that the *paidagōgos* "was often harsh to the point of cruelty, and is usually depicted in ancient drawings with a rod or cane in his hand."[7] As a disciplining pedagogue, the Law constantly struck us with a "rod" of reproof when we fell short of keeping God's standards. And, just as the pedagogue delivered the child to school, so the Law delivered us to the gospel.

---

5. This doesn't mean that people who lived before Christ weren't saved by faith. They were, as Paul has shown us in the example of Abraham. Even under the period of the Mosaic Law, people had to have faith in God to be saved. Paul makes it clear, both in Galatians and Romans, that no one is, or ever was, justified by the Law. The author of Hebrews, too, reminds us that "it is impossible for the blood of bulls and goats to take away sins" and that "without faith it is impossible to please Him" (Heb. 10:4; 11:6a). People in the Old Testament were saved by putting their trust completely in the promises of God, which were foreshadowings of the coming Christ.

6. *The Expositor's Bible Commentary*, vol. 10, p. 467.

7. Stott, *The Message of Galatians*, p. 97.

The Law, then, as a prison and a pedagogue, did its job. It showed us we could never be justified on our own. It showed us that we needed to put our faith in Someone who kept the Law perfectly, Someone who could break the prison bars forever and relieve the pedagogue of his job.

In Christ: Members of God's Family

> But now that faith has come, we are no longer under
> a tutor. (v. 25)

With this verse, Paul transitions from the old life under the Law to our new life in Christ. The dark, dank prison of sin no longer holds us. The incriminating tutor is gone, having been re-placed by a loving Teacher.[8] Or, as Paul says in another letter, "The old things passed away; behold, new things have come" (2 Cor. 5:17b).

We're Now in the Family

Faith in Christ. That's what it takes to be part of God's family. You've probably heard everyone in the whole world referred to as "God's children." But the Bible teaches that there's only one way to enter the kind of relationship with God in which He is our loving Father and we are His sons and daughters—and that is through faith in Jesus Christ.

> For you are all sons of God through faith in Christ
> Jesus. For all of you who were baptized into Christ
> have clothed yourselves with Christ. (Gal. 3:26–27)

Commentator Donald K. Campbell brings out the rich imagery behind Paul's words.

> In the Roman society when a youth came of age he
> was given a special toga which admitted him to the

---

8. This is not to say, of course, that the Law has no place in the life of the believer. Quite the contrary. When we read the Ten Commandments, for example, we desire to live according to God's standards—not to be justified—but because we have already been justified. We long to live righteous lives, to reflect God's goodness, and to do His will—out of gratitude, because we love Him, because we belong to Him, not because we're trying to earn salvation for ourselves. The Law still shows us where we fall short of God's will. But as believers, we can flee to God's grace when we fail, knowing that He accepts us on the basis of Christ's perfect obedience to the Law.

full rights of the family and state and indicated he was a grown-up son. So the Galatian believers had laid aside the old garments of the Law and had put on Christ's robe of righteousness which grants full acceptance before God. Who would want to don again the old clothing?[9]

Paul's reference to baptism in verse 27 doesn't mean we're saved by immersion in water but that we are placed into union with Christ through the baptism of the Holy Spirit, which occurs the moment we believe.

There's more. As Christians, we're not only rightly related to God, we're rightly related to one another.

Unity and Equality in Christ

There is neither Jew nor Greek, there is neither slave nor free man, there is neither male nor female; for you are all one in Christ Jesus. (v. 28)

Just as the Law levels the playing field and excludes everyone as sinners before God regardless of societal position, the gospel welcomes everyone regardless of race or social standing or gender. In Christ, Gentiles and Jews are equally loved and valued by God.

A believing master held no higher spiritual position than the believing slave he owned. And though many men, especially in the Jewish religious system, considered their gender superior in every way, the gospel allowed no room for looking down on women. Gender provides no spiritual advantage. Male and female now stand as corecipients of the grace of God, equally justified in Christ. Stott observes that this great truth

does not mean that racial, social and sexual distinctions are actually obliterated. Christians are not literally "colour-blind," so that they do not notice whether a person's skin is black, brown, yellow or white. Nor are they unaware of the cultural and educational background from which people come. Nor do they ignore a person's sex, treating a woman

9. Donald K. Campbell, "Galatians," in The Bible Knowledge Commentary, New Testament edition, ed. John F. Walvoord and Roy B. Zuck (Colorado Springs, Colo.: Chariot Victor Publishing, 1983), p. 600.

as if she were a man or a man as if he were a woman. Of course every person belongs to a certain race and nation, has been nurtured in a particular culture, and is either male or female. When we say that Christ has abolished these distinctions, we mean not that they do not exist, but that they do not matter. They are still there, but they no longer create any barriers to fellowship. We recognize each other as equals, brothers and sisters in Christ. By the grace of God we would resist the temptation to despise one another or patronize one another, for we know ourselves to be "all one person in Christ Jesus" (NEB).[10]

Heirs of a Promise

Paul closes this section by linking those saved by Christ with God's promise to Abraham.

And if you belong to Christ, then you are Abraham's descendants, heirs according to promise. (v. 29)

This brings us back to the argument at hand. The Judaizers were insisting that the Galatians keep the Law in order to be saved. But this was absolutely unnecessary, since the Galatians were *already* heirs of God's promise to Abraham—the promise of justification by faith (see Gal. 3:6–9).

The time of the prison and pedagogue has passed. Faith has brought us to freedom . . . and family.

Living Insights

Galatians 3:28 has tremendous implications for worship and life in the body of Christ. Take some time to think about how your church is living out the truth of equality in Christ. Is it structured to assemble a group of people who are just like you? Or is it sending a message that a janitor can feel comfortable worshiping alongside the millionaire who owns the building he cleans?

---

10. Stott, *The Message of Galatians*, pp. 100–101.

Are the men the only ones encouraged to use their gifts for the benefit of the body of Christ, or are the women seen as equally valuable?

_____

_____

_____

What about race? Is your church "targeting" a specific racial group, or is it open to people of all races worshiping and serving there?

_____

_____

_____

Is prejudice still tolerated? What steps can you take to move toward living out Galatians 3:28, both as an individual and as part of a church body?

_____

_____

_____

Remember, the gospel isn't just freedom *from* the Law; it's freedom *to* love God and one another.

Chapter 11

NO LONGER A SLAVE—A SON!

Galatians 4:1–11

W ould you rather be a slave or a son? A mere maidservant or a beloved daughter? Would you prefer cleaning a mansion or living in one? Being property or owning property? And if you could choose between watching over a master's estate and inheriting a father's fortune, which would it be? In the profound language of teenage rhetoric . . . duh!

Surely no one would select slavery over sonship, especially after being freed from the former to enjoy the latter. Except maybe the Galatians. Having embraced the gospel, they were no longer slaves under the Law. They were now God's adopted children—free to love Him and others in His family, free to enjoy His boundless blessings, and free to look forward to His sure inheritance.

But the Galatians were buying into the Judaizers' lie that it took more than gracious adoption to be a child of God. You had to *work* your way into the family by keeping the Law. Paul, however, earnestly sought to convince the Galatians that if they accepted the Judaizers' message, they would actually be moving backward into slavery. The Galatians were *already* children of God.

So, building on the theme of sonship he introduced in 3:26, Paul continues his fight to preserve the true gospel and the Galatians' freedom.

Slavery Under the Law

In 3:23–29, Paul described the Law as a prison that held us and a tutor who disciplined us until we put our faith in Christ—until we became "sons" and "heirs according to promise" (vv. 26, 29). This idea of inheritance continues in chapter 4, where Paul again expounds the purpose of the Law but with a slightly different analogy.

> Now I say, as long as the heir is a child, he does not differ at all from a slave although he is owner of everything, but he is under guardians and managers until the date set by the father. So also we,

while we were children, were held in bondage under the elemental things of the world. (4:1–3)

Sons as Slaves?

To understand Paul's imagery, we must first understand the cultural context out of which he spoke. In the first century, "sons were treated as slaves until they received the full rights of sons at the age of maturity."[1] This age, James Montgomery Boice explains, varied, depending on racial and cultural tradition.

> In Judaism a boy passed from adolescence to manhood shortly after his twelfth birthday, at which time he became "a son of the law." In the Greek world the minor came of age later, at about eighteen, but there was the same emphasis on an entering into full responsibility as an adult. At this age, at the festival of the *Apatouria*, the child passed from the care of his father to the care of the state and was responsible to it.
> Under Roman law there was also a time for the coming of age of a son. But the age when this took place may not have been as fixed as is often assumed . . . , with the result that the father may have had discretion in setting the time of his son's maturity. If this is so, it leads one to think that Paul is referring primarily to the Roman custom as he observed that a child is under guardians and trustees "until the time set by his father." A Roman child became an adult at the sacred family festival known as the *Liberalia*, held annually on the seventeenth of March. At this time the child was formally adopted by the father as his acknowledged son and heir.[2]

1. Reprinted from *Galatians* (IVPNTC) by G. Walter Hansen. © 1994 by G. Walter Hansen. Used by permission from InterVarsity Press, P. O. Box 1400, Downers Grove, Ill. 60515, p. 114.

2. Taken from *The Expositor's Bible Commentary*, volume 10, edited by Frank E. Gaebelein. Copyright © 1976 by The Zondervan Corporation. Used by permission of Zondervan Publishing House, p. 471.

"Under Guardians and Managers"

Until that formal announcement of sonship, however, the child was "under guardians and managers," since he was still too young to manage the estate himself. This state of powerlessness made him virtually the same as a slave. Here Paul uses slightly different imagery than he did in 3:23–29. He doesn't liken the Law to a prison or strict disciplinarian but to people who care for and control the child and manage the estate while he is young.

Perhaps Paul shifted to this more positive image of the Law to emphasize God's sovereignty in salvation. Though all unbelievers, like that child, were unable to come into their "inheritance," God was still with them in the form of the Law, which He used to show them their need for Christ.

Even so, life under the Law is still slavery to the "elemental things of the world" (4:3). Some commentators believe this phrase refers specifically to the Mosaic Law, which served as an elementary or introductory phase of the religious life. Though the Law does not save, it does show people what God requires and helps us see our need for His grace.

Some object to this view, though, pointing out that the Galatians were not recipients of the formal Law, as the Jews had been, and did not seek to live by it. However, the Galatians, and all Gentiles, were still obligated to keep God's standards, even if they didn't live under the Mosaic Law as the rule of religion and life. God gave all people an innate sense of right and wrong and has revealed Himself in nature. Therefore, all humanity, Jews with the formal Law and Gentiles without it, are "without excuse" in rejecting Him (see Rom. 1:18–32). We can say, then, that the Galatians were "enslaved" under the Law before coming to Christ in the sense that they knew God existed, but they did not know Him.

Other commentators see these "elemental things of the world" (Gal. 4:3) as objects of idolatrous pagan worship—either the earthly elements (earth, fire, air, and water) or the heavenly bodies (stars and planets). In worshiping the creation instead of the Creator, the Galatians would have been violating God's Law. Being "enslaved" by such false religion, they could not come to God on their own.

Sonship Under Christ

All of us, then, were confined to the custody of the Law, no different from slaves. And God could have left us there. But He didn't.

78

God Sent His Son

> But when the fullness of the time came, God sent forth His Son, born of a woman, born under the Law. (v. 4)

The "fullness of the time" corresponds to the "date set by the father" in verse 2. Donald K. Campbell brings out the connection between these two phrases.

> As a human father chose the time for his child to become an adult son, so the heavenly Father chose the time for the coming of Christ to make provision for people's transition from bondage under Law to spiritual sonship. This "time" was when the Roman civilization had brought peace and a road system which facilitated travel; when the Grecian civilization provided a language which was adopted as the *lingua franca* of the empire; when the Jews had proclaimed monotheism and the messianic hope in the synagogues of the Mediterranean world.[3]

Jesus was "born of a woman," God in the flesh come to live among us. He was also "born under the Law," emphasizing not only that He was born into a Jewish family and subject to the Law, but that He *lived out* the Law perfectly. As Stott writes, "The divinity of Christ, the humanity of Christ and the righteousness of Christ uniquely qualified Him to be man's redeemer."[4]

And that's why He came—to redeem us.

Redeemed and Adopted

> So that He might redeem those who were under the Law, that we might receive the adoption as sons. (v. 5)

To redeem means to buy out of slavery. So Jesus, by His perfect life and sacrificial death, purchased us from the slave block of the Law. Now we're no longer slaves but sons and daughters of God.

---

3. Donald K. Campbell, "Galatians," in *The Bible Knowledge Commentary*, New Testament edition, ed. John F. Walvoord and Roy B. Zuck (Colorado Springs, Colo.: Chariot Victor Publishing, 1983), p. 601.

4. Reprinted from *The Message of Galatians* (BST) by John R. W. Stott. © 1968 by John R. W. Stott. Used by permission from InterVarsity Press, P. O. Box 1400, Downers Grove, Ill. 60515, p. 106.

Because you are sons, God has sent forth the Spirit
of His Son into our hearts, crying, "Abba! Father!"
Therefore you are no longer a slave, but a son; and
if a son, then an heir through God. (vv. 6–7)

Our relationship to God as children is more than a positional
one; it is an experiential one. God gave us His Holy Spirit to seal
our sonship and to give us the ability to call on Him in prayer as
our loving Father[5] (see also Rom. 8:15; Eph. 1:13–14). Paul's mention of the Spirit here also confirms that the entire Trinity—Father,
Son, and Holy Spirit—is involved in salvation. God gave fully of
Himself to bring us into His family.

As God's sons and daughters, then, what are we "heirs" to? Paul
explains in his letter to the Ephesians that God has "blessed us with
every spiritual blessing in the heavenly places in Christ" (Eph. 1:3).
This would include justification, complete forgiveness of sins, un-
limited access to the Father, membership in Christ's church, the
indwelling Holy Spirit, and eternal life.

Why Turn Back?

What riches! And they're all a gift, none of them deserved. The
Galatians had come so far. Once they

did not know God, [but] were slaves to those which
by nature are no gods. (Gal. 4:8)

They had turned from false gods to the one true God. Why,
then, Paul wonders, would they go back?

But now that you have come to know God, or rather
to be known by God, how is that you turn back
again to the weak and worthless elemental things,
to which you desire to be enslaved all over again?
You observe days and months and seasons and years.
I fear for you, that perhaps I have labored over you
in vain. (vv. 9–11)

5. "'Abba,'" says Campbell, "is the Aramaic word for 'Father.' It is the diminutive form used
by small children in addressing their fathers. It is appropriate to see its similarity to the
English word 'Daddy.' Used by Christ (cf. Mark 14:36), this familiar form indicates intimacy
and trust as opposed to the formalism of legalism." "Galatians," *The Bible Knowledge Commentary*, p. 601.

Interestingly, Paul adds "or rather to be known by God," no doubt to emphasize salvation as a work of God and not something that can be obtained by human effort. The "weak and worthless elemental things" are whatever human-centered religious practices the Galatians had observed before coming to Christ.

By following the Judaizers' prescription for worship, the Galatians would be slipping back into slavery. In addition to circumcision, the Judaizers were trying to impose the strict observance of the Jewish calendar on the Galatians (v. 10). The Sabbath, festivals, and celebrations were given by God to keep the Jewish people focused on Him, but they were never meant to save them. By requiring the Galatians to observe these, the Judaizers were adding works to faith as a condition for justification.

So exasperated is Paul with the Galatians that he wonders if he has "labored over [them] in vain" (v. 11). This isn't to say that Paul thought the Galatians who had truly trusted Christ were in danger of losing their salvation. But with the Galatians who wanted to abandon sonship for slavery again, after all they had been given in the gospel, it's easy to see why Paul might have been disappointed that his teaching didn't take them as far as he had hoped. John Stott sums up this section, and perhaps Paul's feelings, this way:

> Oh, the folly of these Galatians! We can certainly understand the language of the Prodigal Son, who came to his father and said "I am no longer worthy to be called your son; treat me as one of your hired servants" or "slaves." But how can anyone be so foolish as to say: "You have made me your son; but I would rather be a slave"? It is one thing to say "I do not deserve it"; it is quite another to say "I do not desire it; I prefer slavery to sonship." Yet that was the folly of the Galatians, under the influence of their false teachers.[6]

Let's not allow the Galatians' folly to become our folly. Let's stop trying to earn the approval of our Father, who has already accepted us—and adopted us—in Christ Jesus. "Abba! Father!" is the cry of sons and daughters, not slaves.

6. Stott, *The Message of Galatians*, p. 108.

This Book Belongs To
G. Kevin Duval

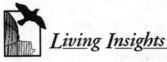 *Living Insights*

Deliverance is one thing; discernment, another. Most of us don't have any problem with believing that Christ died to set us free. We often have trouble, however, staying alert enough to recognize when we're drifting back into bondage.

Why not use this time to take an inventory of how you're doing in the "living free" department. Are you seeking to gain (or retain) righteous standing before God through anything besides the gospel of Christ? Is your pursuit or avoidance of certain activities starting to look more like legalistic requirements than permissible options? Jot down whatever comes to mind.

_____

_____

_____

_____

Have you identified any "weak and worthless elemental things, to which you desire to be enslaved all over again"? Now, what does Paul say is true about you (see Gal. 4:6–7)?

_____

_____

_____

_____

Believe it.

Chapter 12

CARING ENOUGH TO
TELL THE TRUTH

Galatians 4:12-20

Right about now, you might be wondering if Paul is just a distant dispenser of truth and not all that involved with the Galatians personally. Maybe Paul wondered if he was coming across that way too. Because, as James Montgomery Boice points out, the apostle's words now take on a different tone.

> If the reader is inclined to think Paul has been impersonal in dealing with the problems at Galatia, that he has been arguing as a scholar and not as a pastor, the present passage should disabuse him of this idea. It is true that Paul has dealt with the issues facing the Galatians as doctrinal ones and has even been somewhat distant in addressing his converts. The most endearing he has been is in calling them "brothers" (1:11; 3:15), but this was certainly a common enough term within the Christian community. Now, however, all this changes and the deep pastoral concern of Paul for the Galatians, which has stood behind even his staunch biblical and theological discussion, surfaces. In these verses Paul intensifies his appeal to them. He calls them "brothers" once again and then "dear children." The latter, common in John's writings, occurs only here in Paul's.[1]

These verses wedged in the middle of chapter 4 serve as a reminder to everyone who is passionate about championing the gospel: We're to love people as much as we love the truth. When we communicate the gospel, we share it with people—either to those hearing it for the first time or those who have already embraced it. People we want to see living free, rescued from the bondage of legalism. People we want to see enjoying the Christian life to

---

1. Taken from *The Expositor's Bible Commentary*, volume 10, edited by Frank E. Gaebelein. Copyright © 1976 by The Zondervan Corporation. Used by permission of Zondervan Publishing House, pp. 477–78.

the fullest. People we love enough to tell the truth, even if it's hard for them to hear. Ultimately, championing the gospel isn't about our winning or losing arguments. It's about people gaining or losing freedom. Gaining or losing life.

Paul's Personal Plea

As we move into verse 12, Paul goes from proclaiming to pleading.

> I beg of you, brethren, become as I am, for I also
> have become as you are. (4:12a)

This emotional appeal not only tells us Paul's desire for the Galatians, but it also reveals something about his past and present commitment to them. Given the context of the letter, Paul's entreaty for them to become "as I am" probably refers to his desire for them to emulate him in Christian freedom.

"Be free like me," Paul is saying. "Feel the weight of the Law lifted from your life. Get out of that musty prison called legalism. I want you to know what it's like to run unhindered through the sunlit fields of grace—without fear of God's judgment . . . or anyone else's. And I want you to know the freedom of standing for the gospel of Jesus Christ and standing against those who would silence it. Be as I am." That's probably the force of Paul's petition.

Paul knows the Galatians can change, because he became like them ("I also have become as you are"). That is, Paul identified with the Galatians when he first delivered the gospel to them.

> He entered into their culture, adapted to their ways and became one with them. Even though he was a Jew, trained as a Pharisee to be totally separate from Gentiles, he lived like a Gentile in order to reach the Gentiles for Christ. His practice of identification illustrated the principle he enunciated in 1 Corinthians 9:19–22: "I make myself a slave to everyone, to win as many as possible. To the Jews I became like a Jew, to win the Jews. . . . To those not having the law I became like one not having the law . . . so as to win those not having the law. To the weak I became weak, to win the weak. I have become all things to all men so that by all possible means I might save some."[2]

2. Reprinted from *Galatians* (IVPNTC) by G. Walter Hansen. © 1994 by G. Walter Hansen. Used by permission from InterVarsity Press, P. O. Box 1400, Downers Grove, Ill. 60515, p. 132.

Talk about up-close-and-personal evangelism! That's how much Paul loved the Galatians and wanted them to know Christ. So much for any accusations of his being indifferent or not being a people person. If others "are to become one with us in Christian conviction and experience," says John Stott, "we must first become one with them in Christian compassion."[3]

Paul had become like the Galatians so they could hear the gospel. Now he was urging the Galatians to become like him and live the gospel.

Remember When?

Having alluded to his early ministry among the Galatians, Paul decides to linger on the past a bit longer and remind them of how they had welcomed him—and his message.

> You have done me no wrong; but you know that it was because of a bodily illness that I preached the gospel to you the first time; and that which was a trial to you in my bodily condition you did not despise or loathe, but you received me as an angel of God, as Christ Jesus Himself. (vv. 12b–14)

Paul has nothing but good memories about how he was treated by the Galatians. They did him "no wrong" when he first came to their cities with the gospel. Just the opposite: they welcomed him with open arms.

This was particularly memorable for Paul, since he was racked by illness either when he first arrived in Galatia or shortly after. What was Paul suffering from? Various maladies have been suggested. Some commentators have proposed blindness, citing the Galatians' offer to pluck out their eyes and give them to Paul (v. 15). Others have suggested that Paul may have been suffering from malaria or epilepsy.

Whatever Paul's condition, it apparently made him disturbing to look at. His illness was a "trial" for the Galatians and would have caused most people to "despise or loathe" him. But the Galatians did no such thing. On the contrary, they welcomed Paul, showing him the same respect and kindness they would have shown an angel or even Jesus Himself.

3. Reprinted from *The Message of Galatians* (BST) by John R. W. Stott. © 1968 by John R. W. Stott. Used by permission from InterVarsity Press, P. O. Box 1400, Downers Grove, Ill. 60515, p. 113.

Things, however, had changed.

What Happened?

The Galatians' present attitude toward Paul is quite different from their earlier response toward him.

> Where then is that sense of blessing you had? For I bear you witness that, if possible, you would have plucked out your eyes and given them to me. So have I become your enemy by telling you the truth? (vv. 15–16)

This "sense of blessing" probably refers to the Galatians' joy in having Paul around and their appreciation of his ministry. They were so devoted to Paul early in their relationship that they would have "plucked out [their] eyes and given them to [him]." This could support the idea that Paul had some disease of the eye. Or it might be his hyperbolic way of saying that the Galatians would have given their most precious possessions in order to keep him among them, so they could learn from him.

Now, however, the relationship has soured. Paul feels that he is being treated like an enemy. Why? For telling them the truth—that the true gospel, the gospel he teaches, sets people free and that the Judaizers' false gospel enslaves people to the Law.

Paul's situation is so relevant to our day. Teaching the Scriptures often means communicating God's truth to people who don't want to hear it. As G. Walter Hansen notes,

> The dramatic shift from the Galatians' warm welcome to their cold rejection of Paul serves as a sober warning to both pastors and their churches. Pastors should not be so naive as to think they will always receive a warm welcome if they consistently teach the truth. In fact, teaching the truth will always run the risk of alienating some people. And people in the church need to be aware that their initial positive response to pastors who teach the truth will be severely tested when the truth cuts like a two-edged sword. During such a time of conviction, people need to maintain their loyalty to their

pastors precisely because they have the courage to preach the truth even when it hurts.[4]

Paul had the Galatians' best interests at heart. The Judaizers, however, did not.

The Judaizers' Motives

The Judaizers had an agenda. And, as Paul points out, it wasn't an honorable one.

> They eagerly seek you, not commendably, but they wish to shut you out so that you will seek them. But it is good always to be eagerly sought in a commendable manner, and not only when I am present with you. (vv. 17–18)

The Greek word for "eagerly seek" is used in a variety of ways, but the sense here seems to be that of "[launching] an aggressive campaign to win the allegiance of the Galatian Christians."[5] In addition to open attacks against Paul, this probably included insincere flattery. As Stott puts it, "In order to win [the Galatians] to their perverted gospel, the false teachers fawned on them and fussed over them."[6]

Pursuing others and seeking to win them over to your way of thinking isn't bad—as long as it's done "in a commendable manner," that is, with pure motives (v. 18a). After all, that's how Paul pursued the Galatians when he was "present with [them]" (v. 18b). But that's not what the Judaizers were doing. They wanted to shut out the Galatians from their relationship with Paul and their freedom in Christ. The false teachers wanted the Galatians to "seek them," to be under their control and totally dependent on them (v.17). Once again, Hansen makes Paul's warning to the Galatians a warning to us.

> All too often leaders in the church seem to be more interested in the exclusive personal attachment of their followers to themselves than in the spiritual growth and unity of the entire body of Christ. Of course, as Paul admits in verse 18, it is

4. Hansen, *Galatians*, p. 135.

5. Hansen, *Galatians*, p. 136.

6. Stott, *The Message of Galatians*, p. 115.

not wrong to be zealous to win the affection of others, as long as it is for their welfare. But by the very way Paul states this general principle, he calls us to be careful lest we court the affections of others for our own selfish advantage or are courted in such a way ourselves.[7]

Our passion, our goal, as champions of the gospel, should be to bring others closer to Christ, not bring ourselves popularity. That's what drove Paul.

Paul's Passion

My children, with whom I am again in labor until Christ is formed in you—but I could wish to be present with you now and to change my tone, for I am perplexed about you. (vv. 19–20)

"My children." That's a term of endearment, commitment, love—not ulterior motives. Like a mother struggling through labor, Paul wanted to endure this hardship with the Galatians until Christ was formed in them. Paul wasn't interested in just getting them saved and then turning them loose. He wanted to see them shaped into the image of Christ (see also Rom. 12:1–2). He had been "in labor" once before, when he preached the gospel to them. Now he endured labor again as he struggled to see them grow in Christ and be delivered from the false teachers.

Like any loving parent, Paul would rather be present with the Galatians than far away (Gal. 4:20). He would prefer to change his tone from one of rebuke to one of loving instruction. Yet Paul's hard words have been necessary, for he is "perplexed" about their wanting to turn their backs on Christ and live again under the Law.

Sometimes the truth hurts, as they say. But it also sets us free, as Jesus said:

"Then you will know the truth, and the truth will set you free." (John 8:32 NIV)

7. Hansen, Galatians, p. 136.

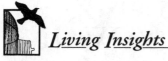 *Living Insights*

Let's face it. Sometimes the truth is the last thing we want to hear, especially if it exposes our spiritual deficiencies. Even when spoken in love by someone who cares deeply about us, the truth sometimes causes us to bristle. The news about ourselves can make us bitter, angry, resentful.

Or it can make us better. It can help us face our weaknesses and help us trust in Christ's life-changing power. Have you heard any hard truth about your life lately from someone who cares about you? Did it sting a bit? What was it?

_____

_____

_____

_____

How did you feel when you heard it?

_____

_____

_____

Has the information helped you in your walk with God? How?

_____

_____

_____

If hearing the truth helped you at all, even if it just caused you to think, why not take a minute to write a note to the person who shared the information with you and thank him or her for loving you enough to do the hard thing.

Chapter 13

TO THOSE WHO WANT
TO BE UNDER THE LAW

Galatians 4:21–31

If you're a lawyer, or if you know anything about the judicial process, you know that it's no fun to lose a case. But it's doubly difficult when your opponent uses your own evidence against you, taking everything you've used to build a solid case, and . . . poof, blowing it down like a house of cards. Suddenly, everything you thought was substantial is now inconsequential. Your ace in the hole is now the opposition's trump card. And the "big guns" you thought you would pull out to wow the jury? They just blew up in your face.

In these last eleven verses of chapter 4, Paul, arguing like a skilled lawyer, will wrap up his defense of justification by faith. And when he's finished, the Judaizers will be picking up cards and wiping gunpowder off their faces for a long time—because Paul is about to use their own evidence against them. He begins with Genesis, the first book of the Law. Then he homes in on Abraham, whose physical descendants, the Judaizers believe, enjoy a spiritually privileged position with God. By the time he's done, Paul has once more shown the superiority of grace over the Law.

The Structure of Paul's Argument

Some commentators consider this section of Galatians the most difficult in the letter. It's rooted deeply in the Old Testament and reflects a rabbinic style of teaching, which is both technical and allegorical.

To help us follow the flow of Paul's argument and interpret the text accurately, John Stott has divided the passage into three sections, or stages:

> The first is historical, the second allegorical and the third personal. In the historical verses (22, 23) Paul reminds his readers that Abraham had two sons, Ishmael the son of a slave and Isaac the son of a free woman. In the allegorical verses (24–27) he

argues that these two sons with their mothers represent two religions, a religion of bondage which is Judaism, and a religion of freedom which is Christianity. In the personal verses (28–31) he applies his allegory to us. If we are Christians, we are not like Ishmael (slaves), but like Isaac (free). Finally, he shows us what to expect if we take after Isaac.[1]

The Historical Stage of Paul's Argument

The Opening Question

Paul begins with a pointed, and somewhat sarcastic, question.

Tell me, you who want to be under law, do you not listen to the law? (4:21)

In essence, Paul is saying, "OK, you Judaizers and all the Galatians who are listening to you. You think that living by the Law is the way to become justified before God? Then listen to what the Law says about itself . . . and see how wrong you are."

The Two Sons of Abraham

Paul directs his readers once again to the book of Genesis and the life of Abraham. As we have noted earlier in this study, nothing made the Jews feel more proud or secure than their descendancy from Abraham. Since they were physically related to the man with whom God made His covenant promises, they assumed that they were "in" with God.

Even before Paul's ministry, though, the Jews were shown to be wrong on this point. When John the Baptizer, the forerunner of Christ, was calling people to repent at the Jordan River, he said to the Pharisees and Sadducees, "Do not suppose that you can say to yourselves, 'We have Abraham for our father'; for I say to you that from these stones God is able to raise up children to Abraham" (Matt. 3:9).

Jesus, too, made it clear that the Jews, just like all sinners, must trust in Him for salvation (see John 8:31–47). Physical connection

---

1. Reprinted from *The Message of Galatians* (BST) by John R. W. Stott. © 1968 by John R. W. Stott. Used by permission from InterVarsity Press, P. O. Box 1400, Downers Grove, Ill. 60515, p. 122.

to Abraham provided no privileged spiritual status before God.

Using the story of the birth of Abraham's two sons, Paul, like John the Baptizer and Jesus, shows the futility of trusting in ancestry, human works, or anything else besides Christ for salvation.

> For it is written that Abraham had two sons, one by the bondwoman and one by the free woman. But the son by the bondwoman was born according to the flesh, and the son by the free woman through the promise. (Gal. 4:22–23)

Though Paul doesn't name them, it's obvious he's talking about Ishmael and Isaac. Ishmael was born by Hagar, a servant of Abraham's wife. He was "born according to the flesh," that is, "in the course of nature and requiring no miracle and no promise of God"[2] (see Gen. 16:1–4a, 15–16). Isaac, on the other hand, was born to the free woman Sarah, Abraham's wife, through God's promise. Isaac was a miracle child, born when Abraham was one hundred years old and Sarah, who had been barren, was ninety. God opened Sarah's womb and brought Isaac into the world, just as He had promised (see Gen. 15:4; 17:15–16; 18:10; 21:1–3).

So, in this brief look at history, Paul sets the slave born by natural means (Ishmael) against the free child born by supernatural means (Isaac). In doing this he illustrates the incompatibility of salvation by natural means (the keeping of the Law) and salvation by supernatural means (the grace of God). In Ishmael and Isaac, Paul provides a picture of what he's been arguing throughout the letter: Salvation comes through faith in Christ alone, not by human effort.

The Allegorical Stage of Paul's Argument

Those claiming special status by virtue of their physical descendancy from Abraham, however, might have viewed Paul's "two sons" account as support for *their* position. Since Isaac was the son of promise, wouldn't the physical descendants of Isaac also be children of promise?

To make his distinction between the Law and grace, and between the Judaizers' "gospel" and his gospel, even clearer, Paul shifts

---

2. Donald K. Campbell, "Galatians," in *The Bible Knowledge Commentary*, New Testament edition, ed. John F. Walvoord and Roy B. Zuck (Colorado Springs, Colo.: Chariot Victor Publishing, 1983), p. 603.

into an allegorical, or symbolic, discussion of the historical events he has just described. This does not mean, Donald K. Campbell writes, that Paul in any way denied

> the literal meaning of the story of Abraham, but he declared that that story, especially the matters relating to the conception of the two sons, had an additional meaning. Thus he compared the narrative to the conflict between Judaism and Christianity.[3]

What Hagar Represents

First, Paul tells us what Hagar symbolizes.

> This is allegorically speaking, for these women are two covenants: one proceeding from Mount Sinai bearing children who are to be slaves; she is Hagar. Now this Hagar is Mount Sinai in Arabia and corresponds to the present Jerusalem, for she is in slavery with her children. (Gal 4:24–25)

Hagar represents the old covenant of the Mosaic Law, given at Mount Sinai.[4] Just as Hagar's son Ishmael was a slave, so those who live under the Law are slaves. Why? Because the Law requires perfect obedience, which no one can attain. Therefore the Law continually condemns us, exposing our sin and keeping us in its oppressive grip. Though Paul doesn't mention it in these verses, the Abrahamic covenant is assumed here as the gracious counterpart to the Mosaic covenant (see Gal. 3).

Hagar also corresponds to the "present Jerusalem" (v. 25). Jerusalem in Paul's day was not only enslaved to Rome, it was enslaved to the Law. Jerusalem was the center of Jewish religion and culture, characterized not by grace but by the slavish pursuit of legalism.

So Hagar the slave and her son Ishmael represent the old covenant of the Mosaic Law as well as Jerusalem, the city of the Law.

What Sarah Represents

Since Hagar represents slavery to the Law, Sarah, as we would expect, symbolizes freedom in Christ.

---

3. Campbell, "Galatians," p. 603.

4. Though Paul doesn't mention the new covenant instituted by Christ, it is implied in the comparison of "two covenants" (Gal. 4:24; see also Jer. 31:31; Luke 22:20).

But the Jerusalem above is free; she is our mother.
(v. 26)

What is the "Jerusalem above"? Remember, Paul is building a contrast here. Hagar corresponds to the literal, earthly Jerusalem, which is inhabited by the Jewish people, who are slaves under the Law. The Jerusalem above, represented by Sarah ("our mother") must, therefore, apply to a nonearthly Jerusalem and all those saved by grace.

Some scholars see this Jerusalem above as the church universal, all those redeemed in Christ. Others see it as heaven, God's dwelling place, which is inhabited by the souls of the redeemed.

Whatever Paul's exact meaning, it's obvious that this "Jerusalem" represents those saved through faith in Christ. It is a place and a people characterized by freedom, not by enslavement to the Law.

Paul shores up his argument for the superiority of freeing faith over enslaving Law by quoting Isaiah 54:1.

> For it is written,
> "Rejoice, barren woman who does not bear;
> Break forth and shout, you who are not in
>   labor;
> For more numerous are the children of the
>   desolate
> Than of the one who has a husband."
> (Gal. 4:25–27)

Isaiah directed his words to the Jewish exiles living in Babylon. He was assuring them that their bondage would not last forever, but that they would return to their homeland and become more numerous than ever.

How, then, is Paul using Isaiah's words to apply to the church? Again, scholars vary. Some believe Paul is saying that God's promise to bless the Jewish exiles and make them fruitful again is fulfilled ultimately in the church, since those in Christ are the "seed" of Abraham (see Gal. 3:16). Others say Isaiah's promise will not be fulfilled until the Millennium. During this time, they say, Israel will again be a great nation, and her Messiah, Jesus, will reign from the earthly Jerusalem.

There's a lot going on in this passage, isn't there? Maybe a more visual representation will help. Let's take a look at a chart of Paul's comparison so far:

Slave or Free?

Hagar, the bondwoman	Sarah, the free woman
Ishmael, a natural birth	Isaac, a supernatural birth
The old covenant of the Law	The new covenant of grace
Earthly Jerusalem	Heavenly Jerusalem
Judaism	Christianity
Slavery to the Law	Freedom in Christ

As you compare these two columns, ask yourself whose child are you?

The Personal Stage of Paul's Argument

If you have put your faith in Christ, you are, like the Galatian Christians, children of the free woman Sarah, children of promise.

Children of Promise

And you brethren, like Isaac, are children of promise. (4:28)

Just as Isaac was supernaturally born as a result of God's promise, so all Christians are "born again" as a result of God's promise to Abraham to bring innumerable spiritual descendants from him. Believers are spiritually to Abraham what Isaac was physically— free children, born as a direct result of God's miraculous intervention.

At Odds with the Other Son

Freedom, however, isn't without friction.

But as at that time he who was born according to the flesh persecuted him who was born according to the Spirit, so it is now also. (v. 29)

Ishmael, as John Stott reminds us, responded to Isaac's favored status by ridiculing the child. And Christians can expect the same treatment from legalists—those enslaved to the Law.

At the ceremony at which Isaac was weaned, when he was probably a boy of three and Ishmael a youth of seventeen, Ishmael ridiculed his little half-brother Isaac. We do not know the details of what happened, because Ishmael's attitude is described by only one Hebrew verb, probably meaning that he "laughed" or "mocked" (Gn. 21:9). Nevertheless, it is clear that Isaac was the object of Ishmael's scorn and derision.

We must expect the same. The persecution of the true church, of Christian believers who trace their spiritual descent from Abraham, is not always by the world, who are strangers unrelated to us, but by our half-brothers, religious people, the nominal church. It has always been so. The Lord Jesus was bitterly opposed, rejected, mocked and condemned by His own nation. The fiercest opponents of the apostle Paul, who dogged his footsteps and stirred up strife against him, were the official church, the Jews. The monolithic structure of the medieval papacy persecuted all Protestant minorities with ruthless, unremitting ferocity. . . . Isaac is always mocked and persecuted by Ishmael.[5]

So, how are we to respond to such persecution?

But what does the Scripture say?
"Cast out the bondwoman and her son,
For the son of the bondwoman shall not be
an heir with the son of the free woman."
(v. 30)

Abraham banished Hagar and Ishmael, remember, because of Ishmael's derision of Isaac. Similarly, Christians today are to reject legalism and refute those who teach it. The Jews, interestingly, interpreted this passage as God's rejection of the Gentiles. But Paul turns the tables, connecting the Jews with the slave woman and all Christians, whether Jew or Gentile, with the free woman.

Paul sums up his whole argument of law versus grace in verse 31:

So then, brethren, we are not children of a bond-woman, but of the free woman.

All who have trusted Christ by faith are free! The judgment's paid. The trial's over. Case closed.

5. Stott, The Message of Galatians, pp. 126–27.

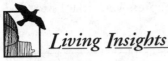 *Living Insights*

Chapter 4 wraps up Paul's formal argument for justification by faith. Before moving into chapters 5 and 6, which focus on the practical outworking of that doctrine, this is a great time to review the main points of Paul's argument. Take some time to read through chapters 3 and 4 and answer the following questions. Then you'll be well on your way to defending the freedom we all hold so dear.

Are justification by faith and our keeping of the Law both legitimate ways to salvation?

_____

Why can't the Law save us?

_____

_____

_____

Why, then, was the Law given, if it was never intended to save?

_____

_____

_____

What images does Paul use to describe our condition under the Law?

_____

_____

_____

What images does Paul use to describe our condition under grace?

_____

_____

Now, what words would *you* use to express your thanks to God for saving you?

_____

_____

_____

_____

_____

_____

_____

Chapter 14

FREEDOM, FAITH, LOVE, AND TRUTH

Galatians 5:1–12

The year was 1934. An impoverished prospector named Jacobus Jonker walked across his small farm in South Africa. The recent heavy rains had washed away loads of silt, and he searched tirelessly for any small treasures the torrents might have turned up. He scurried about, looking high and low for the fortune that would change his life forever. And as he slogged through the mire, Jacobus caught a glimpse of an oddly shaped stone, roughly the size of a hen's egg. As he wiped away the mud, it began to look more and more like a diamond in the rough. Three days later, Jacobus Jonker sold his "rock" for a fortune. It was a 726-carat diamond that became known as the "Jonker diamond," one of the most famous gems in history.[1]

What do you think Jacobus did for the three days before he sold the diamond? What would you have done? You'd be really casual about it, right? Absolutely not. You would do what Jacobus did—everything possible to protect that stone. You'd lock it away in the safest place you could find.

We may not have diamonds equal to the Jonker, but we all have possessions we cherish. And we go to great lengths to protect those valuables. We install security systems in our cars and homes. We buy all kinds of locks and keys to safeguard everything from bicycles to savings accounts. When it comes to our material goods, we play it safe.

We also play it safe when it comes to our spiritual possessions— those convictions and beliefs that are important to us. Whether it's our view of the inspiration of Scripture or our preferred style of worship, we vigorously defend our ideas when someone gives the slightest hint of trying to snatch them away from us.

---

1. Illustration taken from the previous edition of the study guide *Galatians: Letter of Liberation*, coauthored by Bill Watkins, from the Bible-teaching ministry of Charles R. Swindoll (Fullerton, Calif.: Insight for Living, 1987), p. 95. Adapted from Victor Argenzio, *Diamonds Eternal* (New York, N.Y.: David McKay Co., 1974), pp. 50–52.

But there is one spiritual possession we often fail to protect. And, ironically, it is perhaps the most valuable of all our spiritual goods. It's like a spiritual Jonker diamond—so precious that we should hold it close to our hearts and never let it go. It's our freedom in Christ. What do we do to ensure the safety of that freedom? What measures have we taken to safeguard it from spiritual thieves—from legalists?

The Galatian believers gullibly held their freedom with an open hand. They allowed legalistic Judaizers to dupe them out of their liberty and into a yoke of spiritual slavery. In chapter 5, Paul used some of the strongest language in his entire letter to try to get the Galatians to guard their spiritual treasure.

The Statement of Our Liberty

Paul opens with a straightforward declaration:

> It was for freedom that Christ set us free.
> (Gal. 5:1a)

Why did Jesus die on the cross? For one reason, so that we, through faith in Him, could live free from the penalty and power of sin. Once saved, we have no reason to fear God's divine wrath or Satan's supernatural domination. The curse of the Law has been lifted, and we will be spared ultimate judgment for our sin.

This freedom offers us a new kind of life. We have the opportunity to live by the Spirit's power and, as a result, enjoy many benefits. Our freedom gives us the ability to obey God and to do His will joyfully. We can love and serve others as a result of our liberty. We are also able to enter into the Lord's presence through prayer and to strengthen our relationship with Him. Before salvation, we couldn't take advantage of any of these benefits. We were slaves to sin. But now, as free believers, we can enjoy them to their fullest extent. Christ set us free for freedom's sake.

Paul follows his declaration with a command:

> Therefore keep standing firm and do not be subject
> again to a yoke of slavery. (v. 1b)

Why in the world would someone who had been taken from a prison cell to a palace suite want to return to the dungeon? Because our desire to earn our own way is strong. Relying on God's grace seems too easy, so some Christians become slaves under a yoke of legalism by trying to earn God's favor or add to their salvation through good works.

This yoke of legalism can be especially tricky to resist, but understanding how it lures us can help us fight it. Essentially, it can take over our thoughts and actions in two ways. First, by convincing us that good deeds and a pure life are the only ways to become acceptable to God. Second, by turning us into modern Judaizers, convincing other people to strap on the yoke of a works mentality. In either case, Paul's exhortation is the same: Don't do it. Don't give up your freedom. It's a precious gem. Guard it with your life.

The Consequences of Embracing Legalism

What do we stand to lose if we fail to stand for freedom? The next few verses hold the answer.

Christ Will Have No Value

> Behold I, Paul, say to you that if you receive circumcision, Christ will be of no benefit to you. (v. 2)

By receiving circumcision in order to be saved, the Galatians would, in effect, have said that Jesus' sacrifice on the cross was insufficient to save them. They would have been trying to add to His payment for sin. Similarly, when we step toward legalism, we set ourselves up as gods, relying on our own efforts to achieve salvation. By accepting the idea of righteousness by works, we reject the Savior. Consequently, His death is of no benefit to us. From a legalistic point of view, Christ might as well have not come at all. There's no need for Him. Through their actions, legalists say, "We choose the Law, not grace."

We Will Have to Keep the Whole Law

Paul says next,

> And I testify again to every man who receives circumcision, that he is under obligation to keep the whole Law. (v. 3)

The Galatians couldn't choose just one small part of the Law; once they chose any of it, they had really chosen the whole. Likewise, when we reject Christ, we also commit ourselves to earning salvation through the Law. That's a staggering thought. Who of us could obey the whole Law for even a day? Obviously, no one can, except for Christ—and that's why He came. Before we decide to become legalists, we must count the cost.

We Will Be Severed from Christ

In the next verse, Paul issues a sobering warning:

> You have been severed from Christ, you who are seeking to be justified by law; you have fallen from grace. (v. 4)

Commentator Donald Campbell explains Paul's meaning for us.

> Anyone seeking justification by Law has been alienated *(katērgēthēte)* from Christ, that is, such a person would not be living in a sphere where Christ was operative. The KJV has a helpful rendering, "Christ is become of no effect unto you." In addition, said Paul, they would have fallen away from grace. The issue here is not the possible loss of salvation, for "grace" is referred to not as salvation itself but as a method of salvation (cf. 2:21 where "a Law" route is mentioned as an unworkable way to come to Christ). If the Galatians accepted circumcision as necessary for salvation, they would be leaving the grace system for the Mosaic Law system.[2]

Once we choose the Law for our savior, we cut our tie to Christ. We're severed from Him. We have chosen to be justified by our works, thus falling away from grace. But God cannot accept us based on our works. Even our most noble deeds appear as dirty rags to Him (Isa. 64:6). Only the covering Christ provides is sufficient. As legalists who are severed from Christ, we can neither enjoy a right standing before God nor can we grow in Christ.

Contrasts between the Flesh and Faith

What are some differences between living in the flesh and living by faith? First, our approach to personal righteousness is different. When we live according to our own merit, we feel solely responsible

---

2. Donald K. Campbell, "Galatians," in *The Bible Knowledge Commentary*, New Testament edition, ed. John F. Walvoord and Roy B. Zuck (Colorado Springs, Colo.: Chariot Victor Publishing, 1983), p. 605.

for our moral purity. As a result, we feel compelled to work hard for our righteousness. When we live by faith, however, we rest easy, knowing that perfection will come only when Christ glorifies us in heaven. As Paul wrote,

> For we through the Spirit, by faith, are waiting for the hope of righteousness. (Gal 5:5; compare Rom. 8:30; 1 Cor. 15:42–44; 2 Cor. 4:17)

Then, based on Christ's work—and His work alone—we will be made pure and perfect. Think of it: no more pain and suffering, no more temptation and sin. We will be morally, physically, and emotionally perfect, and happier than we could ever imagine. Our own efforts could never achieve such a glorious end.

There's another contrast between the flesh and faith that Paul lays out in Galatians 5:6:

> For in Christ Jesus neither circumcision nor uncircumcision means anything, but faith working through love.

The essential fuel for a flesh-oriented life is works; for a Christ-centered life, it is faith. Not just an intellectual faith, but a practical one that expresses itself in genuine, generous love for others (see also James 1:27; 2:14–17).

The Concern for Those Who Fall from Grace

Paul's approach changes subtly in Galatians 5:7. He shifts from making declarations and commands to asking questions. At the heart of these questions is a deep love and concern for the Galatian believers who had slipped back into slavery. Here he expresses compassion toward and confidence in them and comes down hard on the Judaizers who led them astray. Paul asks four questions designed to get the believers back on track.

Who Tripped You Up?

> You were running well; who hindered you from obeying the truth? (v. 7)

Paul acknowledges that the Galatians had been running well, combining their understanding of grace with a responsible expression of their freedom (v. 7a). But then they stumbled. The imagery here envisions a footrace, not unlike the competitions held in

Greece and Corinth. As the Galatians were running, the Judaizers threw an obstacle in front of them that cut into their stride, hindering their progress (v. 7b).[3] With knees and palms skinned, they left the track. They strapped on a yoke of works, and only grunts and groans could be heard where joy and hope once filled the air.

Paul asked the question because he wanted them to realize the egregious error they were making. Instead of running free toward the crown of life, they were laboriously tilling the fallow ground of fruitless endeavor.

What Effect Is Legalism Having?

God had called the Galatians by grace (1:6). Whoever was encouraging them toward legalism was obviously contradicting God's calling. It certainly wasn't God Himself who was encouraging this change (5:8). So Paul urges them to concentrate on fighting legalism's effects on the community of believers. Legalism's nature is to spread rapidly until it has infected every cell in the church body. "A little leaven," Paul says, "leavens the whole lump of dough" (v. 9). We need, then, to concentrate on preventing legalism's effect on our faith, not on merely hunting down modern-day Judaizers.

Where Will Legalism Lead?

I have confidence in you in the Lord that you will adopt no other view; but the one who is disturbing you will bear his judgment, whoever he is. (v. 10)

Paul expresses confidence that the Galatians will return to grace (v. 10a). He believed that most would shed the Law after hearing about the consequences and his concerns. For those believers who were still unconvinced, Paul's next words about the destiny of all legalists might finally sway them: the Judaizers would be judged (v. 10b). Those who live by the Law will be condemned by the Law (see Rom. 3:20). Legalism leads to judgment, and the only way to avoid that condemnation is to cling to Christ (see Rom. 8:1–2). Paul wanted them to understand where legalism would lead.

Why Am I Still Persecuted?

The Judaizers claimed that Paul actually lived according to the Law. He circumcised Timothy (Acts 16:1–3), and they pointed to

3. John R. W. Stott, *The Message of Galatians: Only One Way*, The Bible Speaks Today Series (Downers Grove, Ill.: InterVarsity Press, 1968), p. 135.

that action as an indication that Paul actually believed and practiced a works mentality.[4] But Paul responded,

> Brethren, if I still preach circumcision, why am I still persecuted? Then the stumbling block of the cross has been abolished. (Gal. 5:11)

The gospel of grace offends human nature because we stoke our pride by believing we can work for anything we want—even heaven. And anyone who pricks that pride with a message of dependence on Christ will catch a white-hot blast of arrogant rage. The fact that Paul was suffering at the hands of the Judaizers proves that he was not on their side. It proves that his message was indeed a gospel of liberty.

Paul's love for the Galatians is demonstrated most clearly in verse 12:

> I wish that those who are troubling you would even mutilate themselves.

Paul would like those preaching circumcision to go emasculate themselves! Sounds really loving, doesn't it? Actually, it carries more concern than we might suspect, as John Stott explains.

> We may be quite sure . . . that it was due neither to an intemperate spirit, nor to a thirst for revenge, but to his deep love for the people of God and the gospel of God. I venture to say that if we were as concerned for God's church and God's Word as Paul was, we too would wish that false teachers might cease from the land.[5]

We might even venture to add to Stott's statement: If all of us were as concerned as Paul was, we would be guarding our spiritual Jonker diamonds with every resource we could find. We would lock our freedom in the deepest part of our hearts and would defend it as vigorously as any other conviction or doctrine. If God wanted it any other way, He would not have given us Galatians 5:1–12.

---

4. Paul had Timothy circumcised out of cultural sensitivity to the Jews, among whom he would be working, not as a requirement for his salvation.

5. Stott, *The Message of Galatians*, p. 136.

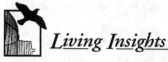

Living Insights

Paul's language in chapter 5 is strong; his argument, convincing. Our spiritual freedom is beyond value, so much more than the Jonker diamond or any other possession. We dare not let it slip away or allow it to be taken from us. Use the following questions to guide you in retaining and exercising your Christian liberty.

How highly do you value your freedom in Christ? List the things in your life that would take precedence over your freedom if you had to choose between the two (money, home, family members, friends, job, reputation, etc.).

_____

_____

_____

Based on what you've learned in this chapter, which of the above items do you feel should be removed from that list?

_____

_____

How strongly do you resist having your freedom stolen? What areas in your life are you currently submitting to legalism?

_____

_____

_____

What can you do to remove those "yokes of slavery"?

_____

_____

_____

How tolerant are you of other Christians and their exercise of freedom? What steps will you take to turn your public policies into personal convictions, allowing others to exercise their freedom in Christ?

_____

_____

_____

How fully do you enjoy the benefits of your freedom? List the ways you serve God and others freely instead of from a sense of compulsion.

_____

_____

_____

In what areas do you still serve grudgingly?

_____

_____

_____

Now that you've examined the value of your spiritual freedom, exercise it! Every day is a new opportunity to live and breathe the liberty Christ has provided. Eugene Peterson exhorts us, "Each day we must take up the stance of freedom again. If we fail to stand deliberately and consciously, the freedom will be lost."[6] Don't lose your freedom. Don't give it away as the Galatians did. Exercise it, and enjoy it.

6. Eugene H. Peterson, *Traveling Light: Reflections on the Free Life* (Downers Grove, Ill.: InterVarsity Press, 1982), p. 145.

Chapter 15

FREE . . . FOR A PURPOSE

Galatians 5:13–15

The first yellow rays of dawn fanned out across the dusky blue Jerusalem sky. Already, Jesus was at the temple, teaching an eager group of early risers. The daylong cacophony of haggling merchants and buyers had not yet dispelled the cool stillness of the morning. Only the warm, resonant sureness of Jesus' voice, along with a few twittering birds in the distance, carried on the air.

Until the scribes and Pharisees hustled in.

Shattering the calm with self-righteous accusations, they strong-armed a desperate woman to the front of the crowd, directly in front of Jesus. "Teacher, this woman has been caught in adultery, in the very act," they underscored. "In the Law Moses commanded us to stone such women; what then do You say?"

At first, He said nothing. He just bent down and wrote something in the dirt. Then, tired of their vicious insistence for a verdict, Jesus stood up. "He who is without sin among you," He said, facing them, "let him be the first to throw a stone at her." Then He quietly resumed writing in the dirt. One at a time, the whole crowd slunk away, until only Jesus and the woman were left.

Standing up, He looked around, asking the woman, "Where are they? Did no one condemn you?" She answered, "No one, Lord." Then, very gently, Jesus granted her her freedom. "I do not condemn you, either. Go now," He said, "and don't let the turkeys get you down. You follow your heart, and you'll be just fine. Believe in yourself, and live the way you choose to live. Bye now!"

What? Wait a minute! That's not how John 8:1–11 ends in the Bible! After freeing her from condemnation, Jesus told her, "Go. From now on sin no more."

God's idea of freedom and our human idea of freedom don't necessarily match. Ours is kind of naive—we see freedom as a casting off of all restrictions, with no particular goal in mind. More often than not, though, our kind of freedom gets us tangled up again in definitely nonfreeing circumstances (commonly called consequences). In contrast, as Paul tells us in Galatians 5:13–15,

God's freedom is purposeful, wise, and truly liberating—with no retanglings and no regrets.

What Freedom Means

God's freedom is a precious gift, yet many of us aren't quite sure what it means. So, before getting into our Galatians passage, let's take some time to define it, exploring what we have been freed from and what we are freed for.

What We Are Freed From

Jesus gave up His glorious life in heaven, His freedom as a member of the Godhead, to secure our freedom. He willingly subjected Himself to the Law, fulfilling it perfectly, and died a terrifying, sacrificial death on the cross. The infinite Source of life was even entombed, until God raised Him from the dead and restored Him to His place in heaven.

Because of His life, death, and resurrection, we are free from God's wrath (Rom. 5:9), the mastery of sin (Rom. 6:22), the dominion of Satan and his demons (Col. 1:13; 1 John 4:4), and living under the curse of the Law (Gal. 3:13). We are free from having to approach God with terror and dread (Eph. 3:12; Heb. 4:16), the condemning accusations of Satan and ourselves (Rom. 8:1), and the tyranny of others' expectations (1 Cor. 10:29b, 31).

God in His grace has done all this for us! But there's more— we are not only set free *from* the restrictions sin shackled us with, we are set free *for* His glorious purposes as well.

What We Are Freed For

God's goal for our freedom is to live as the redeemed people we are. It's as if He has released us from the prison of sin and now we are free—free not to do those things that would put us back in prison but free to live a meaningful life, a beautiful life.

God's freedom takes us to Himself, the One who is Love and Light and Life. It also opens the way to the highest and best in the life He's created us for. Instead of the empty despair of sin, we are called to righteousness and hope (Rom. 6:18; 15:3; 2 Cor. 5:21). Rather than living in grasping selfishness, we are called to open-handed generosity (2 Cor. 9:6–11; 1 Tim. 6:18). Instead of drifting in the haphazardness of our desires, we are directed into the steadiness of God's will (1 Pet. 4:2; 1 John 2:17). Rather than living divided and divisive lives, we are called to be reconciled to God and to be agents of His reconciliation (2 Cor. 5:18–20). Instead of self-centeredness, we are called to care for others (Matt. 25:31–40; 1 Cor. 12:25). Rather than living in isolation, we are called to community (Rom. 12:4–5; Eph. 4:16). Instead of rigid conformity to the world around us, we are called to be transformed into the likeness of the One who is the Way and the Truth and the Life (Rom. 8:29; 12:2).

And the ultimate call of our freedom is not unbridled individualism but holiness and love (John 13:34–35; 1 Cor. 13; 1 Pet. 1:15)—because these represent the ultimate reality Himself.

The Proper Outworking of Freedom

What grand designs God has for us! But what grand messes we so often make of them. We forget what we've been freed from and freed for. We forget what true freedom is and fall back on our false ideas of unrestrained independence, chanting our mantra of "I'll do what I want, when I want."

But that isn't freedom, and that isn't life. And God wants both true freedom and life for His people. Which is why He spoke through Paul in Galatians 5:13–15, reminding us of what freedom—and the Christian life—is all about.

Freedom vs. the Flesh

> For you were called to freedom, brethren; only
> do not turn your freedom into an opportunity for
> the flesh. (Gal. 5:13a)

Paul affirms to the wavering Galatians that they have indeed been freed from the Law. Then, in his next statement, he refutes the Judaizers' accusation that, without the Law, people will become lawless. In doing so, Paul reorients us to freedom's true call with this principle: Christian freedom is not freedom to indulge the flesh[1] (see also 1 Pet. 2:16).

John Stott gives us deeper insight into two key words of Paul's: *flesh* and *opportunity*.

---

1. Reprinted from *The Message of Galatians* (BST) by John R. W. Stott. © 1968 by John R. W. Stott. Used by permission from InterVarsity Press, P. O. Box 1400, Downers Grove, Ill. 60515, p. 140. Chuck Swindoll adapted this section ("Freedom vs. the Flesh") and the next ("Freedom Is Found in Serving") from Stott's fine work on Galatians, pp. 140–42.

"The flesh" in the language of the apostle Paul is not what clothes our bony skeleton, but our fallen human nature, . . . which is twisted with self-centredness and therefore prone to sin. . . . The Greek word here translated "opportunity" (*aphormē*) is used in military contexts for a place from which an offensive is launched, a base of operations. It therefore means a vantage-ground, and so an opportunity or pretext. Thus our freedom in Christ is not to be used as a pretext for self-indulgence.

Christian freedom is freedom *from* sin, not freedom *to* sin.[2]

Sin enslaves us, remember? It leads us into darkness and shame and death. It is insatiable, always wanting something more and something worse. Promiscuity, for example, isn't freedom, even though our society touts it that way. It brings loneliness, emptiness, sometimes disease and abortion. No, sin takes us down destructive paths that wind farther and farther away from the Source of life.

In contrast, Paul tells us a few verses later, "those who belong to Christ Jesus have crucified the flesh with its passions and desires" (Gal. 5:24). Now, our sinful desires don't want to admit that they are dead, so we have to keep reminding them! They are nailed to the cross and no longer have any authority over us.

Freedom Is Found in Serving

You were called to freedom, brethren; . . . [so] through love serve one another. (v. 13)

Being a servant doesn't sound very freeing, does it? Most of us would much rather be the master, having a servant wait on us. We'd like to give the orders. We'd like our needs to be the center of attention. But is that really freedom? Aren't we really bound by the smallness of our own self-interests? Serving out of love, on the other hand, takes us beyond ourselves. It brings us into the fullness of the Father's purpose for our lives. Serving throws open our world and our hearts to care for others.

Paul is reminding us, then, that *Christian freedom is not freedom to exploit others*. As a Christian I have "freedom to approach God

2. Stott, *The Message of Galatians*, p. 140.

111

without fear, not freedom to exploit my neighbour without love."[3] Stott adds that "we are not to use [others] as if they were *things* to serve us; we are to respect them as *persons* and give ourselves to serve them."[4] Serving out of love frees us to respect and restore the dignity of others; it helps us recognize others' God-given value; and it humbles us so that we stop trying to control others and start participating in God's way of doing things.

Freedom and the Law of Love

> For the whole Law is fulfilled in one word, in the statement, "You shall love your neighbor as yourself." (v. 14; see also Rom. 13:8–10)

This is so simple, so basic, and so easily forgotten. Paul reminds us, then, in so many words, that *Christian freedom is not freedom to disregard the needs of others.* We're not to be self-indulgent, using our freedom as an opportunity for the flesh; we're not to be self-serving, exploiting others to accomplish our ends; and we're not to be self-centered, caring only for ourselves and ignoring the good of others. We're to love God and one another, fulfilling the heart of God's Law (see Matt. 22:36–40).

Do you find it curious that Paul suddenly talks of fulfilling the Law here? Throughout his whole letter, he has been establishing that we're free from the Law—is he now putting us under it again? Not at all, as John Stott explains.

> What is the Christian's relation to the law? . . . Our Christian freedom from the law which he emphasizes concerns our relationship to God. It means that our acceptance depends not on our obedience to the law's demands, but on faith in Jesus Christ who bore the curse of the law when He died. It certainly does not mean that we are free to disregard or disobey the law.
>
> On the contrary, although we cannot gain acceptance by keeping the law, yet once we have been accepted we shall keep the law out of love for Him who has accepted us and has given us His Spirit to

---

3. Stott, *The Message of Galatians*, p. 141.
4. Stott, *The Message of Galatians*, p. 141.

enable us to keep it. . . .

Moreover, if we love one another as well as God, we shall find that we do obey His law because the whole law of God—at least the second table of the law touching our duty to our neighbour—is fulfilled in this one point: "You shall love your neighbour as yourself."[5]

Commentator Leon Morris succinctly states: "The rejection of law-keeping as the way of salvation does not alter the fact that the law gives us a useful guide to the way we should live."[6] This doesn't mean that we must now scrupulously obey all of its precepts and prescriptions. Rather, we fulfill its purpose and intent through love: "Love does no wrong to a neighbor; therefore love is the fulfillment of the law" (Rom. 13:10). This law of love is one of God's grandest purposes for setting us free.

Conclusion

In Galatians 5:15, Paul shows us what happens when we revert to our self-oriented, human ideas of freedom.

But if you bite and devour one another, take care that you are not consumed by one another.

A loveless life is a selfish life, driven by clawing competition and cutting criticism. Instead of nourishing each other, we chew each other up; instead of growing together, we shrink into ourselves. As someone once said, "Any man wrapped up in himself makes a very small parcel."[7]

Let's not live small lives, but let's live in the fullness of Christ's freedom. Let's go and sin no more and serve from a heart of love so that the whole world will see Christ and come to Him for real freedom.

5. Stott, *The Message of Galatians*, pp. 142–43.

6. Leon Morris, *Galatians: Paul's Charter of Christian Freedom* (Downers Grove, Ill.: Inter-Varsity Press, 1996), p. 165.

7. As quoted by Morris in *Galatians*, p. 166.

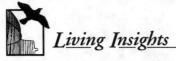

Living Insights

Raw, red scratches. Ragged bite marks. Whole chunks torn away. Tired trails where victor and vanquished dragged themselves away from the contest. What happened? Was it two grizzlies facing off? Two lions in combat for their pride? Two wolves, maybe? No, nothing like that. It was just two Christians biting, devouring, and consuming each other again.

This is what happens when Christians veer off toward self-interest instead of homing in on love. We scratch up each other's psyches with criticism. We sink our teeth into each other's hearts with judgment and contempt. We tear away whole chunks of grace and freedom with condemnation. How pitiful.

Let's spend some time in Romans 14, which is a good complement to our Galatians 5 passage, because there Paul shows us how to let love tame our tearing instincts.

Who are the two groups of believers (Rom. 14:1–2)?

_____

_____

_____

Noting the verbs in verses 3–4 and 10–13a, what do you see these groups doing to each other?

_____

_____

_____

What is Paul's counsel for how the Christian who feels more freedom should relate to the one who does not (vv. 13b, 15a, 20b–22a)?

_____

_____

_____

We could sum up Paul's counsel in this guideline: *When my freedom could hurt my brother or sister, out of love I will yield it.*

Paul's statement in verse 15b offers a bracing dose of true perspective. How would you explain his meaning in your own words?

_____

_____

_____

What does Paul remind us of regarding God's goal for our freedom in verses 17–20a?

_____

_____

_____

A second guideline, then, is this: *When my freedom would hinder God's work because it causes another believer to stumble, I will follow love's lead and yield it for His glory.*

"Love your neighbor as yourself," Paul reminded us (Gal. 5:14). Let's use our freedom, then, to heal wounds instead of inflict them.

 Digging Deeper

Paul was the premier champion for freedom in Christ. But long before he heralded that truth, Jesus Himself taught about the freedom that belief in Him would bring. In fact, our Savior spoke very clearly about how our trust in Him would free us from the flesh, free us to serve, and free us to love—the three areas of life Paul addressed in Galatians 5:13–15. So take some time to hear and reflect on His words and let your life be formed in His freedom.

◆

Freedom from the Flesh

"I tell you the truth, everyone who sins is a slave to sin. Now a slave has no permanent place in the family, but a son belongs to it forever. So if the Son sets you free, you will be free indeed."
(John 8:34–36 NIV)

115

Freedom to Serve

"You know that those who are recognized as rulers of the Gentiles lord it over them; and their great men exercise authority over them. But it is not this way among you, but whoever wishes to become great among you shall be your servant; and whoever wishes to be first among you shall be slave of all. For even the Son of Man did not come to be served, but to serve, and to give His life a ransom for many." (Mark 10:42–45)

Freedom to Love

"A new commandment I give to you, that you love one another, even as I have loved you, that you also love one another. By this all men will know that you are My disciples, if you have love for one another." (John 13:34–35)

Chapter 16

LEARNING HOW TO WALK

Galatians 5:16–25

W e are free in Christ! Paul has taken great pains to emblazon that truth on the hearts and minds of the Galatians. But he has also linked that shining truth to a solemn warning—we can lose our freedom.

If we don't stand firm in the gospel of God's grace, we set ourselves up to "be subject again to a yoke of slavery" (Gal. 5:1). If we use our freedom to indulge our selfish desires instead of loving others, we "turn [our] freedom into an opportunity for the flesh" (v. 13). And with our flesh in control, we're back under the bondage of sin (Rom. 6:16).

How, then, do we keep from wandering off the road of freedom? Paul would answer, "By keeping in step with the Holy Spirit, who guides us along the path of righteousness."

Walking by the Spirit

In Galatians 5:16–25, Paul makes it clear that living free in Christ is centered in the ministry of the Holy Spirit. This section, says Stott, is

> simply full of the Holy Spirit. He is mentioned seven times by name. He is presented as our Sanctifier who alone can oppose and subdue our flesh (verses 16, 17), enable us to fulfil the law so that we are delivered from its harsh dominion (verse 18) and cause the fruit of righteousness to grow in our lives (verses 22, 23). So the enjoyment of Christian liberty depends on the Holy Spirit. True, it is Christ who sets us free. But without the continuing, directing, sanctifying work of the Holy Spirit our liberty is bound to degenerate into licence.[1]

1. Reprinted from *The Message of Galatians* (BST) by John R. W. Stott. © 1968 by John R. W. Stott. Used by permission from InterVarsity Press, P. O. Box 1400, Downers Grove, Ill. 60515, pp. 145–46.

Paul has already explained that life in Christ begins by the Spirit and progresses by the Spirit (3:3). Does that mean we're passive in the process of spiritual growth? Are we supposed to click into a sort of "Holy Spirit cruise control," sit back, and relax? Not at all. Maturing in Christ requires action on our part. It takes discipline. And it doesn't come without a struggle.

That old person we used to be without Christ (the flesh) still tries to gain a foothold in our new life and trip us up, tempting us to trust in the old ways instead of in the Holy Spirit. We're free in Christ. But that freedom is constantly challenged by the flesh. To grow in Christ, then, demands that we take deliberate action. That's why Paul says,

> Walk by the Spirit, and you will not carry out the desire of the flesh. For the flesh sets its desire against the Spirit, and the Spirit against the flesh; for these are in opposition to one another, so that you may not do the things that you please. (vv. 16–17)

"Walk by the Spirit" is another way of saying "Live by the Spirit" or "Let your conduct be directed by the Spirit."[2] Why is the Spirit so vital? As James Montgomery Boice explains, He is "the presence of God in the man, through which fellowship with God is made possible and power given for winning the warfare against sin in the soul."[3] Our flesh, on the other hand, is our fallen selves, "whose desires even at best originate from sin and are stained by it."[4] Quite a drastic contrast between the two, isn't it? As stark a contrast as life and death. Which is why we must consciously yield ourselves to the Spirit, who is our life.

A Continuous Conflict

There is a strain of teaching that claims our sin nature is completely eradicated at conversion and that if we're struggling with

2. F. F. Bruce, *The Epistle to the Galatians: A Commentary on the Greek Text*, The New International Greek Testament Commentary (1982; reprint, Exeter, England: Paternoster Press; Grand Rapids, Mich.: William B. Eerdmans Publishing Co., 1990), p. 243.

3. Taken from *The Expositor's Bible Commentary*, volume 10, edited by Frank E. Gaebelein. Copyright © 1976 by The Zondervan Corporation. Used by permission of Zondervan Publishing House, p. 494.

4. *The Expositor's Bible Commentary*, vol. 10, p. 494. The flesh is also called the "old man," the "natural man," and the "sinful nature."

sin, we must not be truly saved. But Paul's message contradicts such teaching. The struggle between the Spirit and our flesh is unrelenting in this life. The two are "in opposition" to one another, in constant conflict. So fierce is the battle that the flesh sometimes keeps us from doing "the things that [we] please" (v. 17), that is, the good that we want to do (see also Rom. 7).

Rather than being a sign that we're not really saved, our struggle against sin is more likely evidence that we are growing in Christ and that we're striving to do the good that our flesh doesn't want us to do. Otherwise, it wouldn't bother us that our flesh is struggling for control.

The Christian life is a free life, but it is not an effortless life. John Calvin wrote,

> The spiritual life will not be maintained without a struggle. . . . Disobedience and rebellion against the Spirit of God pervade the whole nature of man. If we would obey the Spirit, we must labour, and fight, and apply our utmost energy; and we must begin with self-denial.[5]

We need not despair over this ongoing struggle, however. As the apostle John told us, "Greater is He who is in you than he who is in the world" (1 John 4:4). The struggle should really cause us to depend more and more on God's grace. As Boice says so well,

> Naturally, the flesh is to become increasingly subdued as the Christian learns by grace to walk in the Spirit. But it is never eliminated. So the Christian is never released from the necessity of consciously choosing to go in God's way. There is no escape from the need to depend on God's grace.[6]

Is Paul now putting us back under the Law by prescribing a regimen of deliberate awareness of sin and dependence on the Spirit? Not at all. For

> if you are led by the Spirit, you are not under the Law. (Gal. 5:18)

---

5. John Calvin, *Commentaries on the Epistles of Paul to the Galatians and Ephesians*, trans. William Pringle (reprint, Grand Rapids, Mich.: Baker Book House, 1996), pp. 162–63.

6. *The Expositor's Bible Commentary*, vol. 10, p. 495.

Paul tells us elsewhere, in fact, that we actually carry out the Law when we walk by the Spirit (Rom. 8:4; Gal. 5:14). Following the regimen of the Law and following the leading of the Spirit both require effort. But the only effort that yields true spiritual life is following the Spirit. Just as Christ starts us on our spiritual journey at justification (God's declaring us righteous in Christ), so His Spirit keeps us on the journey in sanctification (the process of growing in Christ). We continue the life of faith as we began it—in the power of the Holy Spirit.

Flesh and Spirit on Display

What, then, does life in the Spirit look like? Surely the Law-seeking Galatians, who were used to assessing life by visible evidence, sought some way to evaluate whether one was living in the flesh or the Spirit. So Paul first supplies them with a catalog of the sins of the flesh; then he sets before them the fruit of the Spirit.

The Deeds of the Flesh

"Now the deeds of the flesh," says Paul, "are evident, which are:

> immorality, impurity, sensuality, idolatry, sorcery, enmities, strife, jealousy, outbursts of anger, disputes, dissensions, factions, envying, drunkenness, carousing, and things like these. (vv. 19–21a)

The phrase "and things like these" shows that Paul didn't intend this list to be exhaustive. Rather, it is representative of the whole spectrum of sinful activity. We won't take time to examine each word in the list, but the fifteen actions can be divided into four main groups: (1) illicit sexual activity, (2) religious perversion, (3) social conflict, and (4) drunkenness.

People who "practice" these actions, says Paul, "will not inherit the kingdom of God" (v. 21b). What does he mean? That true believers can lose their salvation by experiencing a momentary spiritual lapse and acting like nonbelievers? Certainly not; Christ died for all our sins—past, present, and future. And no Christian, not even the most mature, is sinless.

What Paul means is that those whose lifestyles *continually* demonstrate the deeds of the flesh rather than showing the evidence of the Spirit do not have the Spirit. And those who don't have the Spirit will not inherit eternal life.

A word of caution here. It's doubtful that Paul meant for this list to become a foolproof checklist for us to determine with certainty who's saved and who isn't. If we catch someone on a bad day—or a bad week—we could mistakenly evaluate a believer struggling with sin as a non-Christian. We can't look into the souls of others and determine their eternal status. Yet Paul's meaning is clear: These characteristics typify the lives of those who don't know Christ.

The Fruit of the Spirit

Those who do have the Spirit, however, display quite a different set of characteristics.

> But the fruit of the Spirit is love, joy, peace, patience, kindness, goodness, faithfulness, gentleness, self-control. (vv. 22–23a)

Notice that Paul describes the evidence of the Spirit's life as fruit (singular in Greek) as opposed to the deeds (plural) of the flesh. This, says Boice, is an important distinction.

> [Deeds] refers to what man can do, which, in the case of the works of the law (2:16, 3:2, 5, 10), has already been shown to be inadequate. The fruit of the Spirit, on the other hand, suggests that which is a natural product of the Spirit rather than of man, made possible by the living relationship between the Christian and God (cf. 2:20; John 15:1–17). The singular form stresses that these qualities are a unity, like a bunch of grapes instead of separate pieces of fruit, and also that they are all to be found in all Christians. In this they differ from the "gifts" of the Spirit, which are given one by one to different people as the church has need (1 Cor 12).[7]

Though these characteristics defy rigid categorization, some commentators divide them into three triads: inner attitudes sourced in God (love, joy, peace), relational qualities expressed to others (patience, kindness, goodness), and personal qualities that guide individual conduct (faithfulness, gentleness, self-control).

---

7. *The Expositor's Bible Commentary*, vol. 10, p. 498.

It's probably more helpful, though, to see all these qualities as flowing together and flowing out of the believer toward God and others. However we categorize the list, Paul's meaning is obvious: Life in the Spirit means being controlled by the Spirit in every area of life, from our innermost attitudes and emotions to our relationships.

Beautiful fruit is the sign of a healthy tree. But fruit is wasted if it stays on the limb or vine. It is meant to be touched, picked, displayed, smelled, tasted, eaten. Literal fruit only pleases the palate and nourishes the body if it goes beyond the tree. Likewise, the fruit of the Spirit nourishes the body of Christ as we display it in our own lives.

Paul adds,

Against such things there is no law. (Gal. 5:23b)

In other words, the Law can't condemn us when we live in the Spirit. Because when we live in the Spirit, we actually keep the Law (see v. 14). G. Walter Hansen writes,

> There is no rule in the Mosaic lawbook which can be cited against such character qualities. The Spirit-led life is not a life against the law; it is a life that fulfills the law. The way to the fulfillment of the law is not to live under the law like slaves, but to live by the Spirit as children of God.[8]

Practically Speaking

All this begs the question, "How?" How do we walk in the Spirit? How do we keep the flesh from getting a foothold? How do we live a life that consistently reflects the goodness of God? Paul brings this section to a very practical close.

> Now those who belong to Christ Jesus have crucified the flesh with its passions and desires.
> If we live by the Spirit, let us also walk by the Spirit. (vv. 24–25)

Our old nature was crucified with Christ, nailed to the cross with Him (see Rom. 6:6; Gal. 2:20). But Paul reminds us here that

---

8. Reprinted from *Galatians* (IVPNTC) by G. Walter Hansen. © 1994 by G. Walter Hansen. Used by permission from InterVarsity Press, P. O. Box 1400, Downers Grove, Ill. 60515, p. 180.

this is an act we must continue. In verse 24, it is us, not Christ, doing the crucifying. Call it repentance. Call it renunciation of evil. Whatever we call it, it is an act of continually engaging in warfare.

> The fact of warfare against the sinful nature, described in verse 17, indicates that the sinful nature is never fully eradicated in this life and therefore this [saying no to sin] must be continually renewed. But the fact of the execution of the sinful nature described in verse 24 shows that goal of the war against the sinful nature is not a negotiated peace but final execution.
>
> Both the continuous war against the sinful nature and the absolute execution of the sinful nature must be kept in mind if we are to have the full picture. The perfectionists who talk as if the sinful nature has been or can be totally conquered in this life have lost sight of the need to fight the war every day. The pessimists who are halfhearted in battling the flesh because they never expect victory have lost sight of the victory that is ours through active identification with Christ on the cross.[9]

Consciously, consistently saying no to sin. Reminding ourselves of who we are in Christ. Pursuing His will, His life, His glory . . . in His strength. That's what it means to walk in the Spirit. The Holy Spirit came to live with us when we believed, and He is with us for the whole journey ("If we live by the Spirit, let us also walk by the Spirit," v. 25).

 Living Insights

This is that one Living Insights that nobody but you needs to see. Why? Because you're going to get downright personal about sin; you're going to write some of yours down. Well, how about one?

What one "deed of the flesh" seems to be giving you the most trouble? In which area of life does the flesh seem to gain a foothold?

9. Hansen, *Galatians*, p. 181.

Improper sexual desires and actions? Idolatry, perhaps—allowing something or someone to slip into God's rightful place, taking worship away from Him? How about a hot temper? Or overeating? Or overdrinking? Just pick one. And if you plan on giving this guide to someone else after you've read it, write your answer down on a separate piece of paper.

_____

Now, what's your battle plan to start gaining some victory in this area? Can you organize your life to minimize the number of tempting situations you get into? Can you make yourself more accountable? Less secluded? Can you replace a bad habit with a good one? Do you need to change your thinking with the help of key Scripture passages or helpful books? Do you need to break off any destructive relationships or rid your home of some lingering temptations?

_____

_____

_____

_____

_____

_____

_____

_____

_____

_____

_____

Now, give it a try. Be realistic and patient with yourself. And remember, you belong to Christ Jesus and "have crucified the flesh with its passions and desires" (Gal. 5:24).

Chapter 17

RELATING TO ONE ANOTHER IN THE SPIRIT

Galatians 5:26–6:5

What comes to mind when you think of a Spirit-filled church? Signs and wonders? Speaking in tongues?

How about speaking the truth in love? Or gently restoring Christian brothers and sisters who are struggling with sin? Or kindly helping someone grieve during a period of loss and pain? According to Paul, these are sure signs that God's people are walking in the power of the Holy Spirit. Love, gentleness, and kindness, after all, are fruit of the Spirit (Gal. 5:22–23). They are rooted in God, grown in the inner person, and ripened in relationships with others.

You see, Paul knew that the vibrant reality of Christ is meant to be displayed. Contrary to what our individualistic society promotes, the spiritual life is more than an individual experience. It's lived out in community.

Notice, for example, how often Paul and other biblical writers use the phrase "one another" to describe how we're supposed to live out the Christian life. We're commanded to love one another (John 15:12; 1 Thess. 4:9; 1 Pet. 1:22), build up one another (Rom. 14:19), accept one another (Rom. 15:7), care for one another (1 Cor. 12:25), serve one another (Gal. 5:13), bear one another's burdens (Gal. 6:2), be kind to one another (Eph. 4:32), comfort one another (1 Thess. 4:18), and encourage one another (1 Thess. 5:11; Heb. 3:13).

You want to see if the Holy Spirit is at work among God's people? Then take a look at how they treat one another. In Galatians 6, Paul provides practical counsel on humility, gentleness, restoration, and bearing one another's burdens—truth fleshed out in warm and living colors.

How Not to Treat Others

Part of relating to others in the Spirit is knowing what *not* to do. Our passage begins with Paul's negative instruction in Galatians 5:26:

Let us not become boastful, challenging one another, envying one another.

It's no coincidence that this admonition follows verse 25, "If we live by the Spirit, let us also walk by the Spirit." Paul obviously has in mind the opposite of walking in the Spirit in verse 26. Fleshly living is self-centered instead of others-centered, and it is characterized by division instead of unity.

Notice the words Paul uses in verse 26. To "become boastful," says F. F. Bruce, means "to boast where there is nothing to boast about . . . [it] is empty pride or conceit, mere pretentiousness.[1] This would certainly fit with the Judaizers' practice of trumpeting their self-righteous pursuit of the Law as a model of piety. Such practice exalts human effort, but it is empty living. It has no spiritual power. And this would be the Galatians' fate if they continued to follow the Judaizers.

Paul also warns the Galatians to avoid "challenging one another." The image behind this phrase is one of athletic competition—one opponent challenging another to a contest of strength or speed for the purpose of demonstrating his superiority. The Judaizers were no doubt delighting in public debates that showcased their knowledge of the Law and "conformity" to it while intimidating their opponents. They were also drawing Paul into a contest by challenging his message and authority. The Galatians were to avoid this kind of behavior.

While boasting and challenging flow out of feelings of superiority, "envying one another" is rooted in feelings of inferiority. When we're insecure in our gifts, possessions, abilities, and accomplishments, we start to think others are better than we are. So they become the competition instead of brothers and sisters in Christ from whom we can learn.

Neither an attitude of superiority ("I'm better than you and I'll prove it") nor one of inferiority ("You're better than I and I resent it")[2] has a place in the Christian life. Walking in the Spirit fosters an attitude of serving one another, not competing with one another.

1. F. F. Bruce, The Epistle to the Galatians: A Commentary on the Greek Text, The New International Greek Testament Commentary (1982; reprint, Exeter, England: Paternoster Press; Grand Rapids, Mich.: William B. Eerdmans Publishing Co., 1990), p. 257.

2. Reprinted from The Message of Galatians (BST) by John R. W. Stott. © 1968 by John R. W. Stott. Used by permission from InterVarsity Press, P. O. Box 1400, Downers Grove, Ill. 60515, p. 157.

One of building up, not tearing down. Pulling together, not tearing apart.

How to Treat Others

Having provided a snapshot of walking in the flesh, Paul next paints a picture of how to relate to one another in the Spirit.

Restore One Another

How are we to respond to believers who wander from the Spirit's path and stumble into a sinful lifestyle? Legalists would condemn them, but those who follow the Spirit's gracious lead seek to restore them, instructs Paul.

> Brethren, even if anyone is caught in any trespass, you who are spiritual, restore such a one in a spirit of gentleness; each one looking to yourself, so that you too will not be tempted. (6:1)

Restoring sinning Christians to a healthy walk with God can be a sticky issue. On the one hand, many Christians don't feel it's their place to confront anyone about sin. After all, it's a full-time job just to keep ourselves in line, much less tell others how to live. On the other hand, some people think they have been appointed by God to tell *everyone* how to live. They delight in playing the role of the Jesus Police, spying on the body of Christ and itching to interrogate the first saint they see slipping up.

Neither of these extremes is biblical. It is the body of Christ's responsibility to help its members break free from sin's grip. Embracing that obligation is a sign of our love for one another. We're to undertake this responsibility with a spirit of humility and self-evaluation, not haughtiness and self-righteousness.

What, then, should spiritual restoration look like? First, *it is a response to those "caught" in sin.* The language suggests that, rather than nitpicking little offenses, restoration should focus on a sinful situation that has overtaken and is controlling a person.

Who should be doing the restoring? Paul makes it clear that *restoration is to be accomplished by "you who are spiritual."* Who are these? Spiritual giants who have completely subdued the sin nature and are living the perfected heavenly life on earth? Hardly. These are Christians led by the Spirit, who aren't caught in the grip of fleshly living themselves. None of us is sinless—a model of perfect righteousness. But restorers must be mature believers who are producing the fruit of the Spirit in their lives—the love, joy, peace, patience, kindness, goodness, faithfulness, gentleness, and self-control that come from growing in Christ.

Notice, this command isn't limited to pastors, elders, or other officers of the church. Helping Christians through their struggle with sin is the responsibility of the church body as a whole. That means we should all be striving to walk in the Spirit, for we never know when we might be used by God to encourage and help a struggling brother or sister in Christ.

Now we know who is to do the restoring. But *what* exactly are we supposed to do? *We are to restore.* The Greek word for *restore, katartizō,* is used to describe the setting of a fractured bone or the mending of fishing nets. As James Montgomery Boice says, "What is wrong in the life of the fallen Christian is to be set straight. It is not to be neglected or exposed openly."[3] G. Walter Hansen further explains that "the verb *restore* calls for spiritual therapy so that a broken member of the body can once again work properly and perform its vital functions for the benefit of the whole body."[4]

This is a term of caring, healing, mending—not breaking or destroying. Spiritual confrontation is not a way to pay back sinning Christians for all the wrong they've done or to vent our wrath upon them. Not that confrontation is always easy; it can be very unpleasant. But the question is, why are we confronting? Is our goal restoration or revenge? Healing fellow saints or hurting them? Remember, even those caught in sin are human beings with dignity and worth.

How we approach restoration can communicate a lot about what we want it to accomplish. Paul tells us to restore "in a spirit of gentleness." Gentleness, remember, is part of the fruit of the Spirit (5:23). So an individual walking in the Spirit should have this quality. William Barclay illuminates the nature of gentleness for us.

3. Taken from *The Expositor's Bible Commentary*, volume 10, edited by Frank E. Gaebelein. Copyright © 1976 by The Zondervan Corporation. Used by permission of Zondervan Publishing House, p. 501.

4. Reprinted from *Galatians* (IVPNTC) by G. Walter Hansen. © 1994 by G. Walter Hansen. Used by permission from InterVarsity Press, P. O. Box 1400, Downers Grove, Ill. 60515, p. 185.

In the New Testament it has three main meanings. (a) It means *being submissive to the will of God* (Matthew 5:5; 11:29; 21:5). (b) It means *being teachable*, being not too proud to learn (James 1:21). (c) Most often of all it means *being considerate* (1 Corinthians 4:21; 2 Corinthians 10:1; Ephesians 4:2).[5]

True restorers don't descend on other Christians as though they were enemies. They come with compassion in their hearts and concern in their voices. Their words, though firm when they need to be, are laced with kindness and care. And love is never set aside, not even when the hardest truth must be delivered.

Finally, *the restorers, lest they think themselves immune to sin, must look to themselves, so that they too will not be tempted.* Stott explains that restorers must have "a sense of [their] own weakness and proneness to sin."[6] If we have this, we'll have the humility and the dependence on God necessary to help Christian brothers and sisters find their way out of sin.

Bear One Another's Burdens

Helping our Christian brothers and sisters deal with sin is just one way of bearing one another's burdens, a duty Paul urges all Christians to undertake.

Bear one another's burdens, and thereby fulfill the law of Christ. (Gal. 6:2)

Paul's saying that none of us was meant to bear our burdens alone. Life heaps all kinds of unwanted baggage on our shoulders— job stress, deep personal loss, relentless struggles with sin, loneliness, physical pain, divorce, abuse, addiction, and more.

There's no place for an "I can handle this myself" attitude in the family of God. Because we can't. We all need someone to listen to us, talk to us, touch us, encourage us, even confront us. Nor does the superspiritual "I'll just take all my problems to the Lord" disposition get us through. Part of God's plan for lightening our load is to use the hands and backs of His people to help us carry the baggage or show us where we can unload it.

---

5. William Barclay, *The Letters to the Galatians and Ephesians*, rev. ed., The Daily Study Bible Series (Philadelphia, Pa.: Westminster Press, 1976), pp. 51–52.

6. Stott, *The Message of Galatians*, p. 162.

When we bear one another's burdens, we fulfill the law of Christ. That is, we obey Christ's command to love one another (Gal. 5:14; see also John 13:34–35). Quite a different message from the one the Galatians had been hearing from the Judaizers. They heard that righteousness came through keeping the ceremonial Law. But Paul says the opposite. Righteousness comes through faith in Christ and then demonstrates itself through our keeping Christ's law of love. We keep the Law when we walk in the Spirit (see also Rom. 8:4).

The Judaizers sought to burden the Galatians with the Law. But Paul tells the Galatians to relieve each other's burdens and thus fulfill the Law.

In case any of the Galatians consider themselves above bearing the burdens of another, Paul warns,

> If anyone thinks he is something when he is nothing,
> he deceives himself. (Gal. 6:3)

None of us is too good, too spiritual, too "together" either to avoid helping other Christians or resist being helped. The church is a body of believers with diverse gifts, needs, and maturity. We need each other. To think otherwise is to deceive ourselves.

What causes us to think we're too good to bear another's burdens? In a word, pride. We compare ourselves with others and evaluate our spirituality by how much better we're doing than they are. Paul, however, urges us to evaluate our own lives in and of themselves, not in comparison with others.

> But each one must examine his own work, and then
> he will have reason for boasting in regard to himself
> alone, and not in regard to another. (v. 4)

F. F. Bruce explains, "What Paul stresses here is personal responsibility. It is not for one Christian to assess or judge the ministry of another; each one is answerable to God for his own."[7] If we're going to "boast," let us boast in what God is doing through us, not in how much we think we're surpassing other people in spiritual living.

Paul closes this section by circling back to the idea of burden-bearing, but with a slight twist of meaning.

7. Bruce, *The Epistle to the Galatians*, p. 262.

For each one will bear his own load. (v. 5)

Wait a minute. Aren't we supposed to bear *one another's* burdens? Is Paul contradicting what he said in verse 2? Not according to G. Walter Hansen, who sees the two verses as complementary.

> There is no contradiction here with verse 2, which calls for Christians to carry each other's burdens. In fact, Paul uses two different Greek words to make a clear distinction between the *burden (baros)* and the *load (phortion)*. Though these two words are basically synonymous in other contexts, the change of nouns in this context indicates a change of reference. Verse 2 refers to the need to come to the aid of others who cannot carry the crushing burden of the consequences of their sin. Verse 5 refers to work given to us by our Master, before whom we will have to give an account of how we used the opportunities and talents he gave us to serve him. It is because we desire to fulfill our God-given mission in life that we learn how to carry the burdens of others. In other words, as Christians examine their actions to see if they reflect the love of Christ, they are at the same time led by that self-evaluation to consider how to serve others in love.[8]

You want to know if the Spirit is moving in a congregation? Look for burdens shared. That's one clear clue that the Spirit is at work—and that people are walking in step with Him.

 Living Insights

Now that you know that a big part of the spiritual life is helping others bear their burdens (and letting them help bear yours), you might want to take a "baggage" inventory and see if there's an encumbered saint who could use your helping hand. Or you might be the one who needs some relief, and you just need to ask for some assistance.

8. Hansen, *Galatians*, pp. 191–92.

Start with your immediate family and friends. Notice anyone bogged down with discouragement or anxiety? Anyone overwhelmed with just trying to live? Do you see any sinful patterns that are hindering their growth in Christ? What do you see, and what assistance can you offer?

_____

_____

_____

_____

Now, what about other church members, extended family, neighbors, and friends? Any loads you can help carry, even if it's just to help them pray?

_____

_____

_____

Now, how about you? Do you need to swallow your pride and let someone else in on your struggle? Are you weighed down with a sin that you need to confess to God? Do you need to ask His forgiveness, or the forgiveness of someone you've offended? Maybe you just need to open up more—to God, to other Christians—and stop trying to handle it all by yourself. What comes to mind?

_____

_____

_____

_____

Remember, you're a member of the body of Christ. That means no one has to go it alone. Not even you.

Chapter 18

THE LAW OF
THE HARVEST

Galatians 6:6–10

With all that Paul has said about the Law in this letter—it cannot save, it holds people in bondage to sin, it obscures the gospel, etc.—you might get the impression that God's Law is bad. You might even wonder if there's anything good about laws in general. Rest easy. Paul assures us that God's Law, even though it cannot save, is good (Rom. 7:12) and was given for a good purpose (Gal. 3:24).

God has established other good laws, too, as part of His ordering and governing creation. We call them natural laws. Take gravity, for example. Ever broken that one? If so, there's a good chance you broke something else along with it, like an arm or an ankle. If you fall out of a tree or daydream during gymnastics class, the law of gravity will quickly remind you that it must be respected.

Our personal health is also subject to natural laws. For example, if your diet consists mainly of corn dogs, nachos, and ice cream; if you can't remember the last good night's sleep you had; and if your exercise regimen consists of reaching for the TV remote control, you're going to pay with poor health. Maybe not today, but someday. That's just the way the body works.

Through natural laws, God keeps the seasons changing—He thaws the white crust of winter and spins golden raiment for autumn trees. He warms His creation with the sun's light and quenches the parched earth with rain. As God told Noah,

> "While the earth remains,
> Seedtime and harvest,
> And cold and heat,
> And summer and winter,
> And day and night
> Shall not cease." (Gen. 8:22)

The world goes through cycles of change. That's how God set things up.

"Seedtime and harvest" suggests another natural law—one we

133

could call the law of the harvest, which turns seeds sown in the soil into crops to be reaped. This law frames Paul's exhortations in Galatians 6:6–10, where he reminds us to be careful what we sow in the soil of our lives, because we will reap accordingly.

Learning from the Law of the Harvest

The law of the harvest is really a set of four laws. Let's take a quick look at them so we can better appreciate what Paul is saying in this passage.

Law #1: We Sow and Reap in Like Kind

Pretty basic, but important. If you plant watermelon seeds, don't expect a crop of grapes. You don't decide at the harvest what kind of crop you're going to have. It's too late by then. You have to make that decision when you plant the seed.

Law #2: We Reap in a Different Season Than We Sow

Impatient people don't make good farmers. Sun, water, seed, and soil must work together over time to coax crops from the earth. When we sow, then, we mustn't sit with our faces pressed against the window, hoping to see a new crop shoot up overnight. The harvest will come . . . but in another season.

Law #3: We Reap More Than We Sow

Just a handful of seeds yields an abundant harvest of tomatoes. One seed of corn sprouts into a sturdy stalk with multiple ears. And when you plant an apple tree, you get not only the tree but all the apples that tree bears. Seeds are so small; they seem so insignificant, so lifeless. But over time they grow into bountiful crops.

Law #4: We Can Do Nothing about Past Harvests, but We Can Do Something about Future Harvests

What's past is past. We can't change last year's harvest. But we can learn from it. And we can use what we learn to plant wisely now and care for our crop throughout its growth.

By now you've probably already made the connection between agricultural sowing and reaping and spiritual sowing and reaping. If we sow sinful thoughts and actions, for example, we will reap the consequences. And who would argue that many seasons are necessary for the seed of initial faith in Christ to grow into mature Christian fruit?

How else is living the Christian life like raising crops? Let's turn to Galatians 6, where Paul tells us.

Sowing and Reaping in Relation to Financial Support of Pastors

It might surprise you that Paul begins with money. What does paying your pastor have to do with living the spiritual life? Plenty. Because, according to Paul, those teaching the Word of God should be supported by those they teach.

> The one who is taught the word is to share all
> good things with the one who teaches him. (v. 6)

This would have been an especially important admonition to the Galatians. In an environment where the Judaizers were trying to snuff out the light of the gospel, any teachers standing for the truth should be supported financially.

Studying and teaching the Word of God takes time and discipline. Staff pastors, whether they preach each Sunday or prepare curriculum for the youth, shouldn't have to work two jobs in order to make ends meet. A minister should rightly expect to earn a living from the ministry of the gospel.

Are there occasional exceptions? Sure. Even Paul was a tent-maker for a time. But the apostle didn't see his situation as the norm; he encouraged his readers to support those who taught the Scriptures (see also 1 Cor. 9:9–14).

A Warning to Pastors

Does this mean that pastors are free to fleece their flocks? Certainly not. We've all seen preachers and pastors who spend their time doing everything *but* preparing to preach and teach. As a result, the Word is watered down, weakened. Other preachers have no interest at all in rightly dividing the Word of Truth. They want one thing—wealth—and they'll do whatever it takes to get it, even preach falsehood. A person with enough charisma can fool a flock into thinking he's doing God's will. No, Paul has in mind those who work hard at preaching truth (see 1 Tim. 5:17–18)—not twisting it or using it in any way to abuse their congregations.

A Warning to Congregations

Pastors and preachers, however, aren't the only ones who misuse money. Congregations, as John Stott tells us, sometimes use financial leverage to control their pastor.

> Some congregations exercise a positive tyranny over their pastor and almost blackmail him into preaching what they want to hear. They pay the piper, they say; so they must be allowed to call the tune. And if the minister has a wife and family to support, he is tempted to give way. Of course it is wrong for a minister to yield to such pressure, but it is also wrong for a congregation to put him in this predicament. If the minister sows the good seed of God's Word faithfully, however unpalatable the congregation may find it, he has a right to reap his living. They have no authority to dock his wages because he refuses to dock his words.[1]

Pastors aren't puppets to be controlled by congregations, and congregations aren't purses to be plucked by pastors. The pastor and congregation are partners in the same ministry. In fact, the word *share* in Galatians 6:6 contains the same root as *koinōnia*, "fellowship." The pastor shares spiritual wealth with his flock, and the flock shares their material goods with him. Pastor and flock are to look after one another.

An Unchanging Principle

This whole idea of paying our ministers, Paul reminds us, is subject to the law of the harvest.

> Do not be deceived, God is not mocked; for whatever a man sows, this he will also reap. (v. 7)

Though we may fool ourselves into thinking we can ignore the law of the harvest, God cannot be fooled. He has set His natural laws in motion. We sow what we reap. That's a given; that's a principle ordained by heaven.

How does this apply to paying the pastor? It works two ways, really. The pastor sows the Word of God among the congregation, and he reaps not only the blessing of seeing many of them grow in

---

1. Reprinted from *The Message of Galatians* (BST) by John R. W. Stott. © 1968 by John R. W. Stott. Used by permission from InterVarsity Press, P. O. Box 1400, Downers Grove, Ill. 60515, pp. 168–69.

Christ but also the blessing of seeing them commit their resources to the spread of the gospel. Likewise, the congregation sows financial support of the pastor and continues to reap the blessings of the clear and disciplined teaching of the Scriptures. When both pastor and congregation see their relationship in this manner—instead of adversarial or controlling—the way is clear for the gospel to take root and grow in the hearts of God's people.

Sowing and Reaping in Relation to Holy Living

Paul now turns his attention from financial giving to holy living.

> For the one who sows to his own flesh will from the flesh reap corruption, but the one who sows to the Spirit will from the Spirit reap eternal life. (v. 8)

These words of Paul disprove the accusations from his opponents that his gospel promotes loose living. Just the opposite. People saved by grace actually have the power, through the Holy Spirit, to live lives pleasing to God—unlike those who try to please God in their self-righteousness. And the life of faith is anything but passive. It's hard work.

Two Fields, Two Choices

Holy living isn't as mystical as some of us would like to make it. Holiness is a deliberate discipline. Fred Allen once said, "Most of us spend the first six days of each week sowing wild oats, then we go to church on Sunday and pray for a crop failure."[2]

To grow well, we have to sow well. Christians have two fields before them into which they can sow: the field of the flesh and the field of the Spirit. If we're to live a holy life, we must sow in the field of the Spirit. How can we expect to reap a godly life if we neglect the field of the Spirit and instead toss our seed into the field of the flesh. It's the law of the harvest all over again.

Sowing to the Flesh, Sowing to the Spirit

What does it mean to sow to the flesh? It means to pursue thoughts and activities that feed our sinful nature. It's living for short-term satisfaction. This would include such activities as reading

---

2. Fred Allen, as quoted in *Peter's Quotations*, comp. Laurence J. Peter (New York, N.Y.: William Morrow and Co., 1977), p. 108.

137

pornographic literature and indulging other fleshly lusts—but it isn't limited to those. Creating discord in the church is fleshly seed. So is gossip in the workplace. So is laziness. So are harboring grudges, apathy toward the Scriptures, and ignoring the needs of others.

Sowing to the Spirit, then, means pursuing thoughts and actions that produce the fruit of the Spirit—study of the Word, fellowship with other Christians, prayer, corporate worship, speaking the truth in love, self-discipline, caring for the needs of others, and so on.

Stott sums up the truth of verse 8 for us:

> If we sow to the flesh, we shall "from the flesh reap corruption." That is, a process of moral decay will set in. We shall go from bad to worse until we finally perish. If, on the other hand, we sow to the Spirit, we shall "from the Spirit reap eternal life." That is, a process of moral and spiritual growth will begin. Communion with God (which is eternal life) will develop now until in eternity it becomes perfect.[3]

Sowing to the Spirit involves a negative as well as a positive duty. In sowing to the Spirit, we must also *avoid* sowing to the flesh. We must continue to crucify "the flesh with its passions and desires" (5:24) and instead set our minds "on the things above, not on the things that are on earth" (Col. 3:2). Just as harvesting a healthy crop requires that we not only plant seeds but pull weeds, chase off scavenging birds, and destroy ravenous insects, so harvesting a healthy life requires that we identify and root out sinful behavior.

Sowing and Reaping in Relation to Christian Service

We sow what we reap: in financial support of our pastors, in holy living, and in doing good.

> Let us not lose heart in doing good, for in due time we will reap if we do not grow weary. So then, while we have opportunity, let us do good to all people, and especially to those who are of the household of the faith. (Gal. 6:9–10)

We all can lose heart while doing the Lord's work, can't we?

3. Stott, *The Message of Galatians*, p. 171.

Even the Galatians, who heard the gospel truth from the apostle Paul himself, may have become discouraged by the Judaizers' opposition and the kingdom's slow growth. We all can get discouraged when no one notices our contributions; when people stand up and cheer for short-term, worldly accomplishments and ignore the steady, sometimes quiet impact we're making for eternity. Proclaiming the gospel, helping needy people, volunteering our time and energy to the church—these can wear us out, especially when appreciation is seldom voiced.

Paul, however, encourages the Galatians and us to remember the law of the harvest. We will reap, but in a different season. We may not instantly realize the results of what we do in the Lord's name. Sure, we may see someone encouraged by a sermon we preached. We may get to see the joyful, thankful faces of a needy family we helped feed. We may even get to experience the joy of seeing a marriage put back together because of biblical counsel we offered. But some of the results of our efforts we won't see this side of heaven. The traveler who came to faith because we shared Christ with him. The smile on the Lord's face because of the prisoners we visited. Or the legacy of godliness we left behind with our children.

That's why, while we have the opportunity, we should do good to all people, especially those in the family of God. We're to extend Christ's love to all people—not just Christians, yet especially to Christians, since we're all members of the family of faith.

We may have to wait to see the full harvest of all that we're sowing in this life, but we will see it . . . in another season. So don't give up. The Lord knows your work. And He's causing your seeds of service to bear fruit for His glory.

Here's to a bountiful harvest!

 Living Insights

Paying the pastor fair wages. Making deliberate choices that promote personal holiness. Doing good to others in the service of the Lord. Did you catch what these three facets of the Christian life have in common—besides reaping and sowing, that is? How about hard work.

Think about it. The pastor works hard to bring the congregation the Word of Life. The congregation pays the pastor with money they worked hard to make. Denying ourselves and choosing to think and act in ways that help us grow spiritually takes self-discipline. And doing the Lord's work is, well, work. It's especially arduous when the thanks are slow in coming.

The spiritual life is anything but passive. Paul said to the Philippians, "Work out your salvation with fear and trembling; for it is God who is at work in you, both to will and to work for His good pleasure" (Phil. 2:12b–13). God saved us. He is shaping us into the image of His Son. He is maturing us. But that doesn't mean we're a passive member of the process. Yes, it's ultimately up to God whether He allows the farmer's crop to come in. But what farmer would neglect sowing, tending, and reaping—presuming upon God to bring in the crop anyway?

Is there any part of your spiritual life that you've given up on or stopped putting effort into? If so, what is it?

_____

What encouragement can you find in Galatians 6:6–10 to keep tending that crop?

_____

_____

_____

How about sketching out a plan for getting back on track? Maybe you need to enlist the help of an understanding friend or ask your pastor or elders to pray for you. Maybe you need to be more patient with yourself and recognize that gradual progress is still progress. What comes to mind?

_____

_____

_____

_____

_____

You can do it. Stay with it. And remember the law of the harvest.

Chapter 19

A BOLD, BLUNT REPROOF
Galatians 6:11–16

SEE WITH WHAT LARGE LETTERS I AM WRITING TO YOU WITH MY OWN HAND.
(Gal. 6:11)

With these towering words, Paul begins to wrap up his letter to the Galatians. But why the sudden change in penmanship? Why such "large letters"? Some attribute Paul's sprawling handwriting to his poor eyesight. Others propose that he was simply a clumsy, unaccomplished penman. G. Walter Hansen, however, offers a more plausible explanation.

Careful studies of thousands of letters written in Paul's day have led to the discovery that most of the letters exhibit two styles of handwriting: a refined style of a trained secretary in the body of the letter and a more casual style of the author in the conclusion. It appears that it was common practice for letters to be written by dictation to secretaries. The author would personally write only a few lines at the end of the letter. Usually these concluding lines in the author's own hand summarized the cardinal points of the letter. Evidently the author's summary of the main points served not only to verify that he had actually made those points in his dictation to his secretary but also to underline the points he wanted his readers to remember. For this reason the conclusion of a letter often provided important interpretive clues to the entire letter.[1]

1. Reprinted from *Galatians* (IVPNTC) by G. Walter Hansen. © 1994 by G. Walter Hansen. Used by permission from InterVarsity Press, P. O. Box 1400, Downers Grove, Ill. 60515, p. 197.

This practice of using a secretary, or amanuensis, to write letters wasn't unusual for Paul. He employed Tertius in writing Romans (Rom. 16:22). And in some of his letters, including Galatians, Paul made a point of letting his readers know that he himself penned the final greeting (see 1 Cor. 16:21; Col. 4:18; 2 Thess. 3:17).

In Galatians, then, Paul was most likely following the accepted practice of closing out the letter in his own writing. His "large letters" were probably meant to reemphasize his main point, the one truth he didn't want the Galatians to forget: Salvation comes through Christ alone, not through keeping the Law. Where we would use italics, bold letters, or underlining, Paul used larger than normal script.

So, holding up the cross of Christ one last time, and with one final stinging evaluation of the freedom-stealing Judaizers, Paul not only scrawls the gospel on parchment but seeks to imprint it indelibly on the hearts and minds of the Galatians.

All Show and No Substance

Many politicians have been accused of being "all show and no substance." That is, they care more about looking good and maintaining the appearance of significance than they do about actually making a difference. Window dressing. Packaging. That's what such people are about. To them, image is everything.

Religion, like politics, can be approached with a "style without substance" mentality as well. The Judaizers were experts at this approach, as Paul reminded the Galatians.

> Those who desire to make a good showing in the flesh try to compel you to be circumcised, simply so that they will not be persecuted for the cross of Christ. For those who are circumcised do not even keep the Law themselves, but they desire to have you circumcised so that they may boast in your flesh. (Gal. 6:12–13)

By requiring circumcision and ceremonial observance of the Law, the Judaizers were promoting a religion that made people look good on the outside. But the true gospel isn't about mere outward appearances. Christianity makes a difference from the inside out. Why, then, were the Judaizers so intent on making a "good showing in the flesh"?

Running from Persecution

First of all, the Judaizers weren't about to join the ranks of those "persecuted for the cross of Christ." Instead, they paid lip service to Christ but did not actually embrace the Cross—they held to a faith-plus-works system. By not condemning the idea of justification by law, they avoided being persecuted by zealous anti-Christian Jews. The Judaizers were more concerned about preserving their own safety than they were about proclaiming the truth.

Boasting in the Galatians' Flesh

There was a second motive behind the Judaizers' salvation-by-circumcision plan: they wanted to "boast in [the Galatians'] flesh." Hansen explains that the Judaizers

> were not really interested in the moral transformation of the Galatian Christians; they were not teaching circumcision and the law so that Galatian churches would attain new heights of spirituality. Their own inconsistency in following the law demonstrated that devotion to the law was not their basic motivation. What they were really interested in was being able to boast to fellow Jews that they were good Jews. "Look at all the Gentiles we have circumcised and brought into the Jewish nation," they boasted. They sought to earn credit with the Jews by proselytizing the Gentile Christians and forcing them to live like Jews.[2]

Today we're centuries removed from the Judaizers. But we're still tempted to boast in the flesh. One way we do this is by playing the "numbers game"—keeping spiritual statistics so we can feel good about ourselves. How many baptisms, decisions, and rededications can we count? How many people came to this or that church-sponsored event? Whose Sunday school class raked in the most people?

The numbers game is one of the most fleshly games we can play. And, sadly, it's often religious leaders who promote it. That kind of Christianity is external. We need to aim for the hearts and minds of people, not for the tops of growth charts. When we focus

2. Hansen, *Galatians*, p. 199.

on the uncompromising presentation of the gospel, then God alone gets the credit for changed lives and whatever numbers He decides to bring. There's no room for boasting, except in Christ alone.

Boasting in Christ Alone

Having defended that Christianity is primarily an internal matter and is not defined by outward appearances, Paul now takes up the matter of who gets credit for salvation—Jesus Christ or people.

> But may it never be that I would boast, except in the cross of our Lord Jesus Christ, through which the world has been crucified to me, and I to the world. (v. 14)

All Credit Goes to the Cross

Christianity isn't about our achievements. It's not about what we can do for God. It's about what God has done for us. He chose us. He sent His Son to die for us. He gave us new life. It is His power, His grace, that keeps us secure in our salvation. We have nothing to boast about—except the Cross. Every ounce of credit for who we are and for the hope that we have goes to Calvary and to the Savior who died there.

Crucified to the World

Because Paul boasts in the cross of Christ and not in his own accomplishments, he can speak of the world's being crucified to him and his being crucified to the world. John Stott elaborates on Paul's use of crucifixion imagery here.

> As a result [of boasting only in the Cross], we and the world have parted company. Each has been "crucified" to the other. "The world" is the society of unbelievers. Previously we were desperately anxious to be in favour with the world. But now that we have seen ourselves as sinners and Christ crucified as our sin-bearer, we do not care what the world thinks or says of us or does to us.[3]

3. Reprinted from *The Message of Galatians* (BST) by John R. W. Stott. © 1968 by John R. W. Stott. Used by permission from InterVarsity Press, P. O. Box 1400, Downers Grove, Ill. 60515, p. 180.

When the cross of Christ becomes everything to us and the world's approved religion doesn't matter, we can say with Paul,

For neither is circumcision anything, nor uncircumcision, but a new creation. (v. 15)

Fleshly incisions and other religious rituals don't make people right with God. Neither can we trust our salvation to the *avoidance* of such practices. To become children of God we must become new creations (see Rom. 2:29; 2 Cor. 5:17). And the only way to do that is to trust in Christ alone to forgive our sins and make us holy and righteous before God.

A Benediction

What can those who embrace the true gospel and walk by its light expect? Paul's short benediction gives us the answer.

And those who will walk by this rule, peace
and mercy be upon them, and upon the Israel
of God. (v. 16)

Those who "will walk by this rule" are those who accept the gospel and live by it. *Rule* in the Greek is *kanōn*, which literally means "measuring rod." The *canon* of Scripture—the Bible we have today—was assembled by certain criteria or "measuring rods" of authenticity. The Bible is also our *canon* in that it provides God's standards for living. It is also the standard against which all other teaching is measured. Paul is using the word here to apply to the uncompromising truth of the gospel of grace.

Those who follow this gospel can expect mercy and peace. As we've seen already in this letter, the only way to receive God's mercy is through His grace; the Law brings only His judgment. Christ's sacrifice gives us peace with God, changing us from His enemies to His friends. From strangers to family. From objects of His wrath to trophies of His grace.

Christ's salvation also brings mercy and peace because, unlike the Law, Christ's Spirit changes hearts. Now we are enabled to extend God's mercy and peace to others. Because of this, the "Israel of God," the spiritual descendants of Abraham, should be characterized by peace and mercy.

No wonder Paul wrote with such large letters! When we look not only at his epistles but at all of Scripture, the gospel—with its

Christ-exalting, life-changing message—stands out as the defining doctrine of true Christianity . . . and the only hope for humanity. Let us remember it. Defend it. Proclaim it. Live it. Until He comes again.

 Living Insights

Emphasis. That's what Paul's "large letters" were all about. Highlighting the gospel of Christ. Giving it the prominence it was in danger of losing amid a swirl of legalism. To Paul, the gospel was everything. It pervaded his correspondence, his speech, his life. Paul knew that the doctrine of justification by faith alone was the foundational truth upon which all other doctrines stood.

Without the gospel, we have no hope of heaven, no purpose for the church, no standard for living, no reason to preach and teach, no power in worship, no divine help in changing what we don't like about ourselves, no victory over death and Satan. Without the gospel, we are doomed. We are left trying to please God and live for His glory in our own strength, which we are utterly incapable of.

Unfortunately, in many churches, the gospel has been relegated to an insignificant status. Like a campfire in the desert wind, it's fighting to stay ablaze against a gust of programs, politics, entertainment, self-help seminars, Christian celebrity, and heretical teaching.

In other churches, however, the gospel is burning strong and bright. Maybe that's the case where you are. Maybe not. Using Paul's clear portrait of the gospel in Galatians, would you say that the gospel has top billing in your church? How about in your family and personal life?

If so, that's wonderful. If not, what needs to happen to change things? Is it a matter of educating leaders and laity? Refocusing from methods to the message? Taking more time to read and study? Confronting heretical teaching? What would you change?

_____

_____

_____

_____

_____

_____

_____

_____

Jesus said, "I will build My church; and the gates of Hades will not overpower it" (Matt. 16:18b). That means the gospel of grace in Christ will prevail. And who knows? You may be one of those God uses to fan the flame into a full blaze again.

Chapter 20

A BRANDED MAN

Galatians 6:17–18

In the previous chapter, we talked about Paul's passion (and our need) to champion the gospel—to restore it to prominence when legalism, apathy, or ignorance tries to snuff it out.

In these final two verses of his letter, Paul reminds us that such passion for the pure gospel often comes with a price—persecution by those who hate its message of freedom. And Paul should know. His stand for Christ cost him much in terms of personal pain and suffering. Eventually, it cost him his life.

The Command

As he gives the Galatians one final command, Paul obviously hopes they—and the Judaizers—have heard his message loud and clear.

> From now on let no one cause trouble for me,
> for I bear on my body the brand-marks of Jesus.
> (Gal. 6:17)

No More Trouble!

"Let no one cause trouble for me." To whom is Paul speaking here, and what does he mean? Is he telling the Judaizers to stop causing trouble? Although he would like to see their heresy exposed and squelched, Paul most likely doesn't expect one letter to silence them. Legalists dogged the apostle's steps throughout his entire ministry. The party of the circumcision would always be around.

More likely, he's speaking to the Galatians. But what exactly is he saying? Is he instructing them not to bother contacting him if trouble erupts again in Galatia? "I've made my point; now stop bugging me"—that sort of approach? Or is he saying, "You guys just work it out yourselves from now on; I've got other fish to fry"?

Neither. You can bet Paul will want to know whether the words he has sown will take root in soft hearts or bounce off rocky ground. The gospel is at stake; he's not about to pull out of the fight now.

Rather, he's probably telling the Galatians to stop troubling him by entertaining thoughts of giving up the gospel for legalism. The

Galatians' wavering only adds to the suffering Paul has already experienced for the gospel's sake.

Branded for the Cause of Christ

Paul has suffered greatly for championing the grace offered in Christ. His body bears the "brand-marks" of Jesus. The Greek word for these marks (*stigmata*) refers to "signs of ownership such as were branded on slaves and cattle."[1] In 2 Corinthians 11:24–28, Paul catalogs some of the *stigmata* he received throughout his ministry for preaching Christ.

> Five times I received from the Jews thirty-nine lashes. Three times I was beaten with rods, once I was stoned, three times I was shipwrecked, a night and a day I have spent in the deep. I have been on frequent journeys, in dangers from rivers, dangers from robbers, dangers from my countrymen, dangers from the Gentiles, dangers in the city, dangers in the wilderness, dangers on the sea, dangers among false brethren; I have been in labor and hardship, through many sleepless nights, in hunger and thirst, often without food, in cold and exposure. Apart from such external things, there is the daily pressure on me of concern for all the churches.

Paul isn't blowing his own horn or having a pity party in reciting this roster of pain. Rather, these accounts of his suffering accomplish much higher purposes.

First, Paul is backing up his argument for the true gospel with evidence of his willingness to suffer for it. Unlike the Judaizers, who are motivated by self-protection, Paul is prompted by the urgency to declare the truth of salvation in Christ. If his gospel were false, or if Paul just wanted recognition or position for himself, why would he be willing to suffer so much?

Second, Paul's suffering says that he is Christ's slave—devoted to His message and His mission, and driven by His priorities. Just as slaves were branded to show who owned them, Paul had been "branded" to show his allegiance to Christ.

---

1. Donald K. Campbell, "Galatians," in *The Bible Knowledge Commentary*, New Testament edition, ed. John F. Walvoord and Roy B. Zuck (Colorado Springs, Colo.: Chariot Victor Publishing, 1983), p. 611.

And third, this idea of a physical mark on the body lampoons the Judaizers' requirement of circumcision for salvation. It's as though Paul is saying, "You want physical signs to show that I belong to Christ; I'll show you some. My back bears the scars of persecution for the gospel's sake."

The Benediction

Having fired that final volley against the legalists, Paul concludes his letter on the same note he began: grace.

> The grace of our Lord Jesus Christ be with your spirit, brethren. Amen. (Gal. 6:18)

James Montgomery Boice ties together these last two verses and crystallizes the essence of the entire epistle:

> Paul's legacy is, therefore, a wish that the grace of God would be increasingly realized and that whatever external marks there might be, would be received, not as an effort to impress God ritualistically, but as a natural result of true Christian service. The church will always know great days when these are the two distinguishing marks of God's people.[2]

Grace. Lavished on the soul by Christ. Lived out in service to His glory. That, in summary, is the gospel. And that is why we no longer need shackles. In Christ, we are free. Let us live free.

 Living Insights

Way to go! You've studied the entire letter to the Galatians. Before leaving this study, though, why not take one last Living Insight to help solidify the epistle and its major truths in your mind? The following questions will help you think through the three major sections of the letter and blend its truth into everyday life.

---

2. Taken from *The Expositor's Bible Commentary*, volume 10, edited by Frank E. Gaebelein. Copyright © 1976 by The Zondervan Corporation. Used by permission of Zondervan Publishing House, p. 508.

Chapters 1–2: The Personal Section

Paul spent the first two chapters of Galatians defending his authority as an apostle and upholding his gospel as the true gospel. As you think through his approach, how important would you say your reputation is to your impact for Christ?

_____

_____

_____

Why would Paul, who eschewed the "favor of men" (1:10), care what people thought of him? Why didn't he just go straight into the doctrine of justification by faith instead of spending two chapters defending his apostleship?

_____

_____

_____

When should we be willing to defend our reputation? Every time someone speaks ill of us? Whenever we want our way? When honor for honor's sake is at stake?

_____

_____

_____

Chapters 3–4: The Doctrinal Section

Having read Paul's clear distinction between the Law and the gospel, can you differentiate between the two? Give it a try, using the following questions.

Why is Paul's discussion of the Holy Spirit so important to understanding the difference between the Law and the gospel?

_____

_____

_____

Which came first in history, the promise of salvation or the Mosaic Law?

_____

What is the purpose of the Law, and why can't it save us?

_____

_____

What was our status before we came to faith in Christ?

_____

_____

What is our status now that we have placed our trust in Christ?

_____

_____

Chapters 5–6: The Practical Section

The gospel, Paul tells us in this final section of his letter, isn't just head knowledge. It affects how we live. What does the gospel free us *from*?

_____

_____

What does the gospel free us *for*?

_____

_____

How does the fruit of the Spirit differ in appearance from the works of the flesh?

_____

_____

_____

152

_____

_____

List some ways you can "bear one another's burdens" (6:2) in your sphere of care and influence.

_____

_____

_____

_____

_____

We're glad you joined us for this study of Galatians. We hope you've come to love and appreciate your freedom in Christ—and the Christ in whom you are free—more deeply. And may you, like Paul, never forget the price at which your freedom came—the death of "the Son of God, who loved [you] and gave Himself up for [you]" (Gal. 2:20b).

BOOKS FOR PROBING FURTHER

A s you've seen in this study, those who want to walk in Christian freedom will have that freedom challenged and threatened by legalists. That means we must always keep the grace of God in Christ before us. We must know the difference between law and grace, between human effort and Christ's work on the cross, between living to please people and living to please God.

So, just in case you're tempted to try on those shackles again, we suggest you strengthen your resolve to stay on freedom's path with the help of the following books. Consider them guides to a grace-filled life. Flares that lead you back to freedom if you wander into legalism. And keys that will always fit those cold, heavy shackles.

Commentaries

Campbell, Donald K. "Galatians." In *The Bible Knowledge Commentary*. New Testament edition. Ed. John F. Walvoord and Roy B. Zuck. Colorado springs, Colo.: Chariot Victor Publishing, 1983.

Gaebelein, Frank E., ed. *The Expositor's Bible Commentary*. Vol. 10. Grand Rapids, Mich.: Zondervan Publishing House, Regency Reference Library, 1976.

Hansen, G. Walter. *Galatians*. The IVP New Testament Commentary Series. Downers Grove, Ill.: InterVarsity Press, 1994.

Stott, John R. W. *The Message of Galatians: Only One Way*. The Bible Speaks Today Series. Downers Grove, Ill.: InterVarsity Press, 1968.

Other Helpful Books

Bloesch, Donald G. *Freedom for Obedience: Evangelical Ethics in Contemporary Times*. San Francisco, Calif.: Harper and Row, Publishers, 1987.

Deiter, Melvin E., Anthony A. Hoekema, Stanley M. Horton, J. Robertson McQuilkin, and John F. Walvoord. *Five Views on Sanctification*. Grand Rapids, Mich.: Zondervan Publishing House, Academie Books, 1987.

Horton, Michael. *Putting Amazing Back into Grace*. Grand Rapids, Mich.: Baker Book House, 1994.

Luther, Martin. *The Bondage of the Will*. Trans. James I. Packer and O. R. Johnston. Grand Rapids, Mich.: Baker Book House, Fleming H. Revell, 1957.

Martin, Walter. *The Kingdom of the Cults*. Revised and expanded edition. Minneapolis, Minn.: Bethany House Publishers, 1985.

Packer, J. I. *Keep in Step with the Spirit*. Old Tappan, N.J.: Fleming H. Revell Co., 1984.

Sproul, R. C. *Faith Alone: The Evangelical Doctrine of Justification*. Grand Rapids, Mich.: Baker Book House, 1995.

Stott, John R. W. With a study guide by Lance Pierson. *Christian Basics: A Handbook of Beginnings, Beliefs and Behaviour*. Grand Rapids, Mich.: Baker Book House, 1991.

———. *The Cross of Christ*. Downers Grove, Ill.: InterVarsity Press, 1986.

Swindoll, Charles R. *The Grace Awakening*. Dallas, Tex.: Word Publishing, 1990.

Some of the books listed may be out of print and available only through a library. For those currently available, please contact your local Christian bookstore. Books by Charles R. Swindoll may be obtained through Insight for Living, as well as some books by other authors. Just call the IFL office that serves you.

Insight for Living also has study guides available on many books of the Bible as well as on a variety of topics, Bible characters, and contemporary issues. For more information, see the ordering instructions that follow and contact the office that serves you.

NOTES

NOTES

NOTES

NOTES

NOTES

ORDERING INFORMATION

GALATIANS

If you would like to order additional study guides, purchase the cassette series that accompanies this guide, or request our product catalogs, please contact the office that serves you.

United States and International locations:
Insight for Living
Post Office Box 69000
Anaheim, CA 92817-0900
1-800-772-8888, 24 hours a day, 7 days a week
(714) 575-5000, 8:00 A.M. to 4:30 P.M., Pacific time, Monday to Friday

Canada:
Insight for Living Ministries
Post Office Box 2510
Vancouver, BC, Canada V6B 3W7
1-800-663-7639, 24 hours a day, 7 days a week

Australia:
Insight for Living, Inc.
General Post Office Box 2823 EE
Melbourne, VIC 3001, Australia
(03) 9877-4277, 8:30 A.M. to 5:00 P.M., Monday to Friday

World Wide Web:
www.insight.org

Study Guide Subscription Program

Study guide subscriptions are available. Please call or write the office nearest you to find out how you can receive our study guides on a regular basis.

Monday	September 14	**No Longer a Slave — a Son!** Galatians 4:1 – 11
Tuesday	September 15	**Caring Enough to Tell the Truth** Galatians 4:12 – 20
Wednesday	September 16	**Caring Enough to Tell the Truth**
Thursday	September 17	**To Those Who Want to Be Under the Law** Galatians 4:21 – 31
Friday	September 18	**To Those Who Want to Be Under the Law**
Monday	September 21	**Freedom, Faith, Love, and Truth** Galatians 5:1 – 12
Tuesday	September 22	**Freedom, Faith, Love, and Truth**
Wednesday	September 23	**Free . . . for a Purpose** Galatians 5:13 – 15
Thursday	September 24	**Free . . . for a Purpose**
Friday	September 25	**Learning How to Walk** Galatians 5:16 – 25
Monday	September 28	**Learning How to Walk**
Tuesday	September 29	**Relating to One Another in the Spirit** Galatians 5:26 – 6:5
Wednesday	September 30	**Relating to One Another in the Spirit**
Thursday	October 1	**The Law of the Harvest** Galatians 6:6 – 10
Friday	October 2	**The Law of the Harvest**
Monday	October 5	**A Bold, Blunt Reproof** Galatians 6:11 – 16
Tuesday	October 6	**A Bold, Blunt Reproof**
Wednesday	October 7	**A Branded Man** Galatians 6:17 – 18
Thursday	October 8	**A Branded Man**

Broadcast schedule subject to change without notice

Insight for Living • Post Office Box 69000, Anaheim, CA 92817-0900
Insight for Living Ministries • Post Office Box 2510, Vancouver, BC, Canada V6B 3W7
Insight for Living, Inc. • GPO Box 2823 EE, Melbourne, VIC 3001, Australia

Printed in the United States of America

INSIGHT FOR LIVING

Broadcast Schedule

Galatians: Letter of Liberation

August 17–October 8, 1998

Monday	August 17	**Set Me Free!** A Survey of Galatians
Tuesday	August 18	**Set Me Free!**
Wednesday	August 19	**Another Gospel Is Not** *the* **Gospel** Galatians 1:1 – 10
Thursday	August 20	**Another Gospel Is Not** *the* **Gospel**
Friday	August 21	**A Radical Transformation** Galatians 1:11 – 24
Monday	August 24	**A Radical Transformation**
Tuesday	August 25	**A Gospel Worth Accepting and Affirming** Galatians 2:1 – 10
Wednesday	August 26	**A Gospel Worth Accepting and Affirming**
Thursday	August 27	**Confronting Hypocrisy** Galatians 2:11 – 16
Friday	August 28	**Confronting Hypocrisy**
Monday	August 31	**The Exchanged Life** Galatians 2:17 – 21
Tuesday	September 1	**The Exchanged Life**
Wednesday	September 2	**Backsliding into Legalism** Galatians 3:1 – 9
Thursday	September 3	**Backsliding into Legalism**
Friday	September 4	**Delivered from a Curse** Galatians 3:10 – 14
Monday	September 7	**Delivered from a Curse**
Tuesday	September 8	**A Promise You Can Count On** Galatians 3:15 – 22
Wednesday	September 9	**A Promise You Can Count On**
Thursday	September 10	**From Law to Faith: Our New Status in Christ** Galatians 3:23 – 29
Friday	September 11	**From Law to Faith: Our New Status in Christ**